My prayer for you reading this book —

May you find rest and solitude in Him.

May you find your missing puzzle piece, your purpose and identity.

May you truly experience the unconditional love of the Creator within the pages of this book.

Amelia
xx

ROOTED IN LIFE - The power of a sound mind.

Copyright© 2021 by Amelia Mathee

All rights reserved. This book is protected by the USA, UK and international copyright laws. This book may not be copied or reprinted for commercial gain or profit. The use of short quotations or occasional page copying for personal or group study is permitted and encouraged. Permission will be granted upon request.

Published by Seraph Creative in 2021
United States / United Kingdom / South Africa / Australia

Typesetting & Layout by Feline
www.felinegraphics.com

Printed in USA, UK and RSA, 2021

All rights reserved. No part of this book, artwork included, may be used or reproduced in any matter without the written permission of the publisher.

ISBN (Print) 978-1-922428-38-7

DISCLAIMER: THIS BOOK DOES NOT PROVIDE MEDICAL ADVICE.
Its purpose is to give valuable insights into mental health from a Biblical perspective, and is for your general knowledge only. It should not be used by you or any other person to make a diagnosis on your health. The information, including but not limited to, text, graphics, images and other material contained in this book are for informational purposes only. This material is not intended to be a substitute for professional medical advice, diagnosis or treatment. Always seek the advice of your physician or other qualified health care provider with any questions you may have regarding a medical condition or treatment and before undertaking a new health care regimen, and never disregard professional medical advice or delay in seeking it because of something you have read in this book.

ROOTED
IN LIFE

The power of a sound mind

AMELIA MATHEE

Published by Seraph Creative

Rooted in Life Therapy Reviews

"After looking at the in-depth work Amelia did with a wide range of clients, I decided to book a session with her myself. I am a pastoral psychologist and therapist with decades of service in the field of severe psychological trauma and have found what Amelia does—at the level and depth of the service and love she gives to people—as remarkable. She is able to show someone without an 'identity' and even disabilities how loved they are. I have found her sessions to be groundbreaking in my own life and so much more than speaking to a 'normal psychologist' ... Lastly I want to mention that I have studied in depth in the area of psychology and come to the conclusion that Amelia would have to have been called by God with what God enables her to do through His Spirit. She helps to free people from years of torment in their minds and never says no to help.

I have found her heart to be pure, as she was stripped of all dogmas in how she should be working and lives in total dependence from God who she loves so much. He called her and qualified her to do the impossible."

- Dr. C van denBerg

"I started having sessions with Amelia during a time when I was on a suicide path. Her gentle approach absolutely saved my life. She listens without any judgment. During sessions with her, she helped me to look at things and situations differently. When the same darkness came over me, I immediately knew where to go. God's forgiveness, peace, and love shines through her. Amelia has a gift and that gift absolutely saved my life."

- Izzy   (Cape Town, South Africa)

"After only two sessions my view of myself and others has changed. Coming to the realization that I'm full of negative thoughts and the power they have in the outcome of my relationships and life was staggering. That was the first step for me: realization and consciousness of my thoughts ... Having a vision of Jesus inside of people helped my vision of myself and others. Mindset change!! My heart softened and my thoughts are becoming more loving . It takes work to stop those fire breathing negative beasts (thoughts) ... I love how you put Jesus into these teachings along with the science He works through and within us. He is in me, now let Him shine through me. The light of love—words can't explain enough the new vision I have! Thank you, precious sister in Christ, for healing the heart and mind."

-Anne (Iowa, USA)

"It's funny how our own minds can trick us to cover up our thought life—we think we know something, but it turns out that deep down we believe something entirely different. I could quote all the Bible verses about love, yet somehow didn't feel loveable. Amelia helped to expose all the wrong core beliefs preventing me from healing and began to instill a healthy theological foundation. She helped me find that "green pasture" in which I can lie down, rest, and be at peace with my Father. When your mind can finally function from a place of love, everything else falls into place."

- Lesley (Minnesota, USA)

"I approached Amelia Mathee last spring to help coach me through a very stressful school year and to help coach me so I could balance my work life and personal life. Amelia coaches with Cognitive Behavior Therapy. Through different strategies, she has taught me how not to sweat the small stuff, how not to be offended by others, how to usher in the presence of the Lord in my work, and how to challenge and bust negative thinking. Amelia, thank you for pouring your coaching expertise on me. I intend to use this in my day-to-day life. It has helped me cope through this COVID season. Thank you, dear sister, from the bottom of my heart."

- Anna-Marie, a K-8 certified ELL teacher and mother of an energetic 8-year old (Seattle, USA)

"In a world that is so fast-paced and that teaches you to do things separate from God, all of which puts you in unrest and short-circuits your mind, it's refreshing to read Amelia's book. It will teach you how to live in the freedom that God has given you. The cognitive exercises get your mind and focus where they need to be. Thank you for the truths and understanding—the tools we need to receive healing and freedom on our own and maintain it."

- Kelly (Minnesota, USA)

Acknowledgements

I have had so many people and organizations who have encouraged me along the way to a Sound Mind, and as we are many parts within His body, I feel it is only my privilege and honor to acknowledge those who made such an impact on changing my Mind about who God is.

First of all, I want to thank the One who made this all possible, My Lord and Savior. He has truly walked with me every step I've taken, and He continues to guide me and instruct me.

I want to thank the early church Fathers, even though they are not here anymore. Although this book may be controversial to some reading it, I want to remind you that this really is old school, not modern evangelical.

All the medical experts who have guided me and taught me.

Insight from Dr. Christa Van den Berg and Dr. Michelle Strydom.

To my family who were patient when I got "lost" in my work.

To my parents who were always there when I needed them.

To all the people who came into my office and made a positive change to their mental health.

A special thanks to each person who contributed their artwork to this book. Many of the drawings featured are done by clients who use art to express their inner world.

Thank you to Lesley Rieland who is a close friend and a brilliant author. Thank you for crossing my t's and dotting my i's, and for all the work you've done in this book. Thank you for every idea, thank you for late nights and time spent away from family. Thank you for who you are. Thank you. Thank you. Thank you.

Please be sure to check out Lesley's book, *My Kiss Won't Miss*. While the message of my book is ultimately to encourage you that you are not separated, her book does so in few enough words for children, yet deep enough content for even us adults. Nothing can separate you from His love. Nothing.

I also want to express my gratitude for resources such as: Trinitarian theology

Trinity in you (fb)

Trinitarian Theology forum (fb)

Perichoresis.org

Table of Contents

Introduction		12
Prologue:	From Death to Life	14
Chapter 1:	Our Neuron Trees	17
Chapter 2:	Be the Tree You're Meant to Be: Radical Self-Acceptance	25
Chapter 3:	Body, Soul, and Spirit Connection	33
Chapter 4:	The Cognitive Model: Tapping Into Our Brain Trees	39
Chapter 5:	Renewing of the Mind	49
Chapter 6:	Rest in this Truth: You are Accepted, Not Separate	59
Chapter 7:	Cognitive Distortion	71
Chapter 8:	Perception	81
Chapter 9:	The Waymaker	91
Chapter 10:	The Family Tree: Our Purpose and Calling	101
Chapter 11:	The Darkness of Dualism	109
Chapter 12:	The Puzzles of Our Life	117
Chapter 13:	Anxiety	127
Chapter 14:	Hopelessness	137
Chapter 15:	Anger Management	141
Chapter 16:	Obsessive Compulsive Disorder	147
Chapter 17:	Depression: The Big Black Dog	155
Chapter 18:	Toxic Relationships	163
Chapter 19:	Self-Destructive Behavior	175
Chapter 20:	Self-Care	179
Chapter 21:	Happiness	187
Chapter 22:	Quantum Entanglement	193
Chapter 23:	Build Resilience	197
Chapter 24:	He Swallowed Death in Victory	205
Endnotes		216
About the Author		219

Introduction

"For God has not given us the spirit of fear, but of power and of love and of a sound mind."

(2 Timothy 1:7)

My passion for those who struggle mentally grew from compassion. In order for me to help them, I had to try and understand what they were going through. This book is not only for those who struggle with severe mental challenges, but to everyone who struggles somewhere in life with their thoughts.

You were created to have a sound mind, which encompasses your whole frame of thinking, including your rationale, emotions, and cognitions. Every part and process of the human mind can be of sound mind. I have seen many, many people transformed by the tools in this book, and I aim to train more people in this very exciting field of psychotherapy.

Today, I am a Cognitive Behavior Practitioner and I have my own practice in Cape Town, South Africa. I see people from all walks of life, different backgrounds, different races, different ethics, but they all have one thing in common—the Light and Love of the Creator shines through them all. Some shine bright, some very dim, and there are those who don't even know they shine. Now before you stop reading this, let me assure you—I am *not* a universalist. I have no time for universalism. You will not be standing in front of a heavenly electric gate, but in front of a Person. He will either say *I knew you* or "*I never knew you*" (Matthew 7:23). It won't be based on reconciliation or works, it will be based on a relationship.

By merging what God has done in and through my life with my knowledge of secular counseling practices and an understanding of the brain, I have been able to help many people that could not be helped by any other form of medical intervention. Countless hours of study and picking the brain of professors in neuroscience has made this book possible. I have always been fascinated by the brain, the connection to our mind and what role the Spirit plays in all of this.

A note to all reading this: As a disclaimer, this book is intended for your general knowledge only. Its purpose is to give valuable insights into mental health from a Biblical perspective. It is not intended to serve as a substitute for a consultation and proper care by a medical doctor. It should not be used by you or any other person to make a diagnosis on your health. You should seek prompt medical attention for any mental health problems, rather than assume that you can use my teachings as a substitute for proper medical care. This book is intended as supplementary encouragement, education, and exercise on your journey to healing. I am not a medical doctor, so if you have a mental disorder, please seek professional help with a therapist for diagnosis and treatment. Please do not stop your medication, I will not be held liable for any death or injury in any form whatsoever.

What I want to achieve in this short course is to show you the connection between the mind and the Spirit, and how to change your mental health for the better. It is important to note that the chapters build upon one another, so please do not cherry pick specific ones while ignoring others. I don't want you to miss out on any foundational context that may be missed if you skip ahead. I want you to get the big picture!

I would like to show you that everything is connected, and that when you play the script till the end you realize that He is wonderfully and majestically interwoven into our very being. The Tree of Life runs through all of Creation, sustaining all and maintaining all. His roots are well grounded, embedded, intertwined and inextricable.

PROLOGUE

The Tree of Life

It happened on a Friday, the 14th of July in 1995. I was traveling with my family, sitting comfortably in the back seat of our car. A conversation had begun between my mother and I concerning a family member, and I remember the sadness that had come over me. It had become a religious debate. I may not have known much, but I knew God must have been something ... something more.

I had looked out the window at the passing trees, pondering who God really was, sensing He was much bigger than we could ever imagine. The trees were a picture of beauty, swaying in the wind as we sped by them, great poplar trees bending back and forth from the wind. Little did I know what an immense effect trees would have in my life. Now, the vision of the trees are forever cemented in my mind.

There must have been a crashing sound, or a jolt, though I don't remember hearing or feeling anything. A car had suddenly driven into the side where I was sitting, sending our car into a roll. Once it came to a standstill, my mom had looked at me, saw that I was blue and that I had stopped breathing. In a panic my parents tried to get me out, but the car had caved in. I was stuck. My dad eventually broke through the car window and was able to pull me out.

In the midst of their trauma, I was in a peace I had never experienced before. Walking in green pastures, I remember the sweet smell of flowers blooming and the sound of ... Life. It is hard to explain. On my left was the most beautiful man wearing a white robe and smiling. He picked me up, carried me around, and showed me how lovely everything was that *He* had created. Our interaction felt so comfortable, so natural. I wasn't wondering what He thought about me. I wasn't wondering whether I was acting the way I should in front of Him. I wasn't unsettled, nor striving. I was not trained in scripture or brainwashed. I was just simply *being*.

Lastly, He brought me before the most lofty, beautiful tree.

I remember slowly opening my eyes from the coma and feeling great sadness sweep over me. I felt ... heavy. I'd suffered a traumatic brain injury from the severe impact to the left side of my skull. I couldn't move my limbs. I could not talk. No one understood me. My eyes had not adjusted, so everything was blurry. And the most jarring... I could no longer see the shining man with the white robe. Yet, amidst all of this, I could still feel the peace of His Presence for days after I had awoken.

And so my journey began.

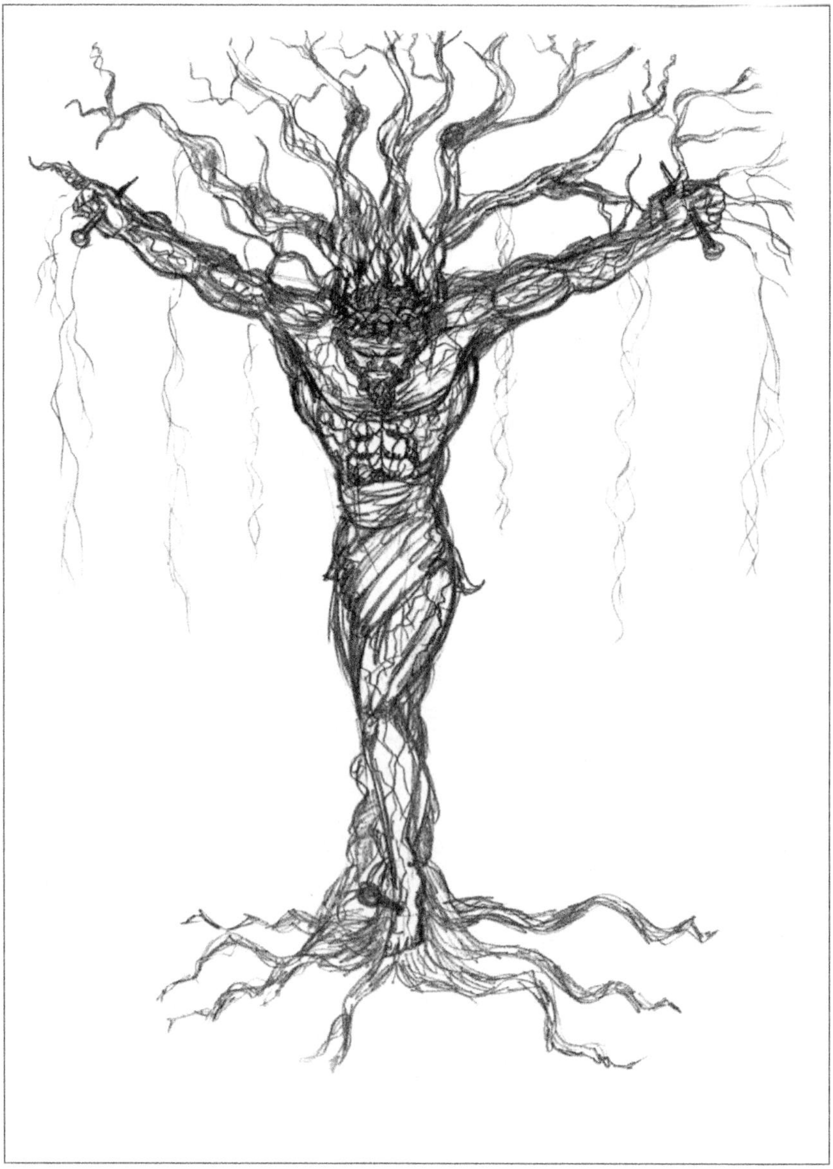

CHAPTER 1

Our Neuron Trees

"Because information processing in the brain is fundamentally a matter of circuitry, we can truly say that the trees of the brain are the roots of the mind."

Giorgio A Ascoli, Trees of the Brain,
Roots of the Mind

The more I read and study the human body, our thought processes, and the way we are wired, I stand amazed at the Beauty of the Creator. We are not merely star dust floating around aimlessly, and I hope to prove this to you. The Bible would have had to be written by the Creator, the One who knows exactly how we are made. There is no other explanation.

If we were to enlarge a human brain a thousandfold, at first glance it would look like a tree with intricate branching. These nerve trees are beautiful and awe-inspiring, and they enable us to move, feel, love, and enjoy life. We take in information with our five physical senses, and this information is stored somewhere in the midst of our trees.

One of the aspects of cognitive psychology I find most fascinating is the fact that we are all so different! We all have different mental filters through which information runs. Our filters are things like our past, our biases, or our fears, and because we are all unique, so will our output be. You can have two people look at the same object, yet come to completely different conclusions. For example,

I can give you a certain brand of biscuits (aka cookies, for you Americans) and to you it will be just a box of biscuits. To me? It will remind me of my mom and how she would buy me that specific brand of biscuits whenever I left home.

Every day our senses take in information. We may see that particular brand of biscuit, smell a specific perfume, taste that bit of cinnamon in the tea, feel the cold floor under our feet, or hear a dog barking. Most of this information is forgotten. What we are most likely to remember are the things which have elicited an emotional response in the past.

If I asked you what you ate yesterday, you might not remember. However, what if I asked about that specific dinner when you received the call that a friend or relative died? The emotional response connected to that meal makes it more likely to be remembered. Furthermore, memories created with each sense will become a filter for our responses in the future. We connect emotions to our senses.

Just last week, I was in the bath and opened a new bottle of shower gel. As soon as I smelled it, I began having flashbacks of my 14-year-old self in a hospital bed being washed by my mom. In an instant I was there again. You, on the other hand, may use the same shower gel and to you it would be lovely.

The nerves, or rather our trees, are information messengers. It's because of these little guys that you are able to wink, smile, and twitch. Your brain is basically made up out of a collection of nerves. As we go through life, we take in information. It goes from our external world to our internal world through our senses. Your brain has to be able to process the information coming in, and how it does that is by building branches on the nerves in your brain. A new branch is being made to hold information, and this is where your memory is.

As you think on a particular thought for a prolonged period of time, the branches on your memory trees will begin growing, and thus the memory becomes stronger. The more you think about it, the stronger and more permanent the memory becomes. The more branches you have on a particular nerve, the stronger the memory is.

The brain is equipped with so many processors, it may be capable of executing 100 billion operations per second[1], but you will be surprised to know that you may only be conscious of only 50 bits per second or less[2]. We were made by an intelligent Creator who knows how we are wired.

The average human brain has 100 billion nerve cells[3] (that's quite a forest). Some neuroscientists believe that you have 300 years worth of storage space in your brain[4] ... so keep on studying!

ARE WE GROWING A BRAIN TREE OF LIFE OR DEATH?

> *"I call heaven and earth as witnesses today against you, that I have set before you life and death, blessing and cursing; therefore choose life, that both you and your descendants may live"* (Deuteronomy 30:19).

God made us in His image, and we have the mind of Christ, so think about everything that He did. God gave us an incredible brain, and we should learn to use it. What if you were able to change the way you think and physically heal yourself? Not in some 'over the rainbow' or 'think happy thoughts' kind of way, but truly changing the chemistry in your brain which in turn promotes health and wellbeing ... *what if*?

Medical science has proven that a very high percentage of diseases originate in your thought life. What kind of memories are you building on your branches? Do they contribute to your health or are they harming it? The quality and information stored on your branches depends on your thought life. Are you building good memories that are good for you, or are you building toxic memories that contribute to you getting sick?

If you are meditating on emotions such as fear and anger, then your brain is full of toxic memories which in turn create toxicity in your body and will eventually make you sick. When you think about this, toxic memories are physically being built into the nerve network of your brain.

Let me share a quick rundown of several key parts of your brain and why they are so important:

Corpus Callosum: We use a specific part of our brain to analyze and think. The corpus callosum is hypothesized to play a primary role in cognition. It connects your left hemisphere and your right hemisphere so that they can communicate.

Cortex: This is where the trees of one's mind are located. Everything we've done from birth to our last breath will be stored in the cortex on these trees. This is your grey matter.

Parietal Cortex: The parietal cortex is part of the cortex. New research suggests that this part of our brain functions as our free will. Here is where we make associations and where we decide to act.

Hypothalamus: The hypothalamus serves as our mind-body connection. This area of the brain converts everything going on in one's thought life into a physical reaction in the body.

These messages come from our external world where it's filtered through our mental filters. It will travel through various areas in the brain, until it gets to our free will. This is the area where we have the ability to either accept or reject a thought - the ability to "take every thought captive" and essentially choose between life-giving thoughts or ones which bring death. Finally, the thoughts we choose to accept have a connection to and will have an effect upon our physical bodies.

Let's use an example:

Emily grew up in an abusive home. It didn't seem to matter how hard she tried, her parents were never happy with her, and they made sure to let her know it. Any mistake (or perceived mistake) would be met with enraged screaming, name-calling, and physical intimidation or violence. She never knew when and what would set them off next.

Recently, Emily began employment at a local business. The first time Emily hears someone raise their voice at her job, she might get anxious or fearful. She might even feel like a trapped child.

Will Emily:

A: Be scared and get out of the building ASAP?

or

B: Acknowledge that her brain is a map of the past, and she is no longer a prisoner?

Which is a healthier reaction, choice A or choice B?

Many people feel like they are a slave to their fears, their past traumas, or disappointments. I want to offer encouragement. My reason for introducing you to different parts of the brain is not because the different scientific names bear any importance to healing. Rather, it is to encourage you that science reveals the amazing journey we can initiate to rewire our brains, create healthy thought processes, and thus heal our mind-body connection. Today, we have the science to show us, and even before this neuro-scientific stamp of approval, we had scripture encouraging us that this journey to healing is indeed possible.

WHERE SCRIPTURE MEETS SCIENCE

"For the weapons of our warfare are not carnal but mighty in God for pulling down strongholds, casting down arguments and every high thing that exalts itself against the knowledge of God, bringing every thought into captivity to the obedience of Christ,"

(2 Corinthians 10:4-5).

The Bible refers to strongholds at least 50 times. It is commonly referred to as a fortress with difficult access. If I had a fortress around me, I would be able to protect myself. However, what if instead of protecting me, that very stronghold prevents me from seeing God for who He is? What if my view of God is tainted by things like tradition, religion, or man-made ideas? How will my outlook change? This stronghold will then be the very structure the enemy will use to blind me. I believe I've been wrong for most of my life concerning what a stronghold is; I was looking at the demonic, assuming that the stronghold was built up of spiritual forces that need to be defeated. Today, I see it quite differently. I see strongholds in the form of lies, manipulations, and distorted thinking.

When we choose with our free will to believe a certain thought, our bodies will respond to that thought. When we think about fear or anxiety, our bodies will release chemicals that make us sick. Our bodies will release certain chemicals in either excessive or insufficient quantities and because it's done in incorrect quantities, it changes the structure of the memories built in your brain. Meditating on a toxic thought will make that toxic thought stronger, and its effects on you will become all the more destructive.

The good news is that the same process occurs with a healthy memory. Neuroplasticity is the brain's superpower to remodel, change and reorganize. When you meditate on good things, the branches on those trees will cause the release of healthy chemicals— serotonin, endorphins, and dopamines. These hormones uplift you, make you feel good, and bring about healing. Recent medical research indicates that if you "bathe" in this daily, it brings about physical health. These findings are consistent with what the Word says.

Proverbs 4:20-22 states:

> "My son, give attention to my words; incline your ear to my sayings. Do not let them depart from your eyes; keep them in the midst of your heart; for they are life to those who find them, <u>and health to all their flesh</u>. Keep your heart with all diligence, for out of it spring the issues of life."

Your emotions and behaviors do not stand isolated, they are in fact a product of your thoughts.

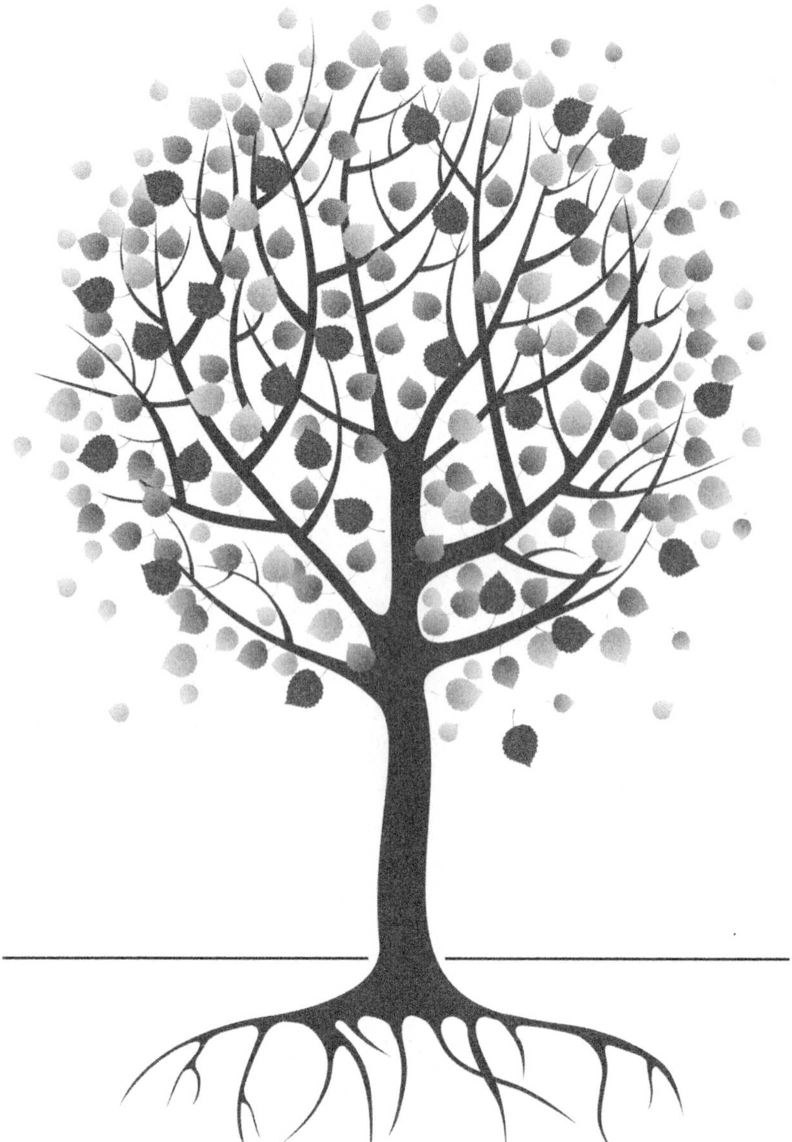

CHAPTER 2

Be the Tree You're Meant to Be:

RADICAL SELF-ACCEPTANCE

> *"He shall be like a tree planted by the rivers of water, that brings forth its fruit in its season, whose leaf also shall not wither; and whatever he does shall prosper."*
>
> (Psalm 1:3)

Scripture often refers to us as trees. In Mark 8:24, Jesus was healing a man of blindness. As this man was gaining sight, he looked around and described what he saw: "I see men like trees, walking."

The Lord also showed Ezekiel trees in a vision. He described what he saw as follows:

> "When I returned, there, along the bank of the river, were very many trees on one side and the other... Along the bank of the river, on this side and that, will grow all kinds

> of trees used for food; their leaves will not wither, and their fruit will not fail. They will bear fruit every month, because their water flows from the sanctuary. Their fruit will be for food, and their leaves for medicine" (Ezekiel 47:7,12).

You are the fruit tree. You are unique and beautiful. We are all different fruit trees, and we carry different fruits. We all carry the essence of who He is, the great Gardener. As it says in John 15:1, "I am the true vine, and My Father is the vinedresser."

Very interesting how Psalms compare us to trees, and that in Ezekiel it speaks of the trees with leaves for healing. Revelations 22:1-3 reveals the same:

> "And he showed me a pure river of water of life, clear as crystal, proceeding from the throne of God and of the Lamb. In the middle of its street, and on either side of the river, was the tree of life, which bore twelve fruits, each tree yielding its fruit every month. The leaves of the tree were for the healing of the nations. And there shall be no more curse."

If the branches/leaves are for the healing of the nations, then God cares more about what is going on in our minds than we think. Jesus makes it very clear that He cares more about what is on the inside, and that what is on the inside will find its way to the outside. "Blind Pharisee, first cleanse the inside of the cup and dish, that the outside of them may be clean also" (Matthew 23:26).

It comes down to this. We need to give thought to what we are thinking about. We need to become aware of our unconscious thoughts and behaviors. How are we speaking? How are we acting? If you look at the emotions you live with everyday, have you simply become used to it? Have particular emotions become so familiar that you just think it's you? It's time to identify what's the real you versus what you're allowing to identify you.

Many, many different trees and many different fruits. We are all so unique. It's meant to be that way. Each of us has different gifts and they all work together in the body of Christ. Yet, how many times have you looked at someone and imagined it could be you?

Wished it could be you? You can try and copy them, but if you don't get the "act" right, will you blame yourself, or perhaps blame God? Or perhaps you're good at the act, but will it feel right? Can living in a mask really be satisfying? Somewhere deep down, your true design may be crying out. Will you then walk the path He has planned for you?

Let me give you an example. The Salvator Mundi is a painting made by Leonardo da Vinci and was sold for $450.3 million[1]. Salvator Mundi' is a Latin phrase, and it means 'savior of the world'. It is part of Christian iconography and depicts Jesus giving a benediction (blessing) with his raised right hand with three of the fingers unfolded, symbolizing the Trinity. What if I were to make a copy of it and print it? Would it be worth anything? No, it's the original painting which holds great value, and this is what is important.

I remember watching a final episode of Survivor. I was struck by a woman whose name was Sarah. Sarah had good values and was very kind. She was in the police force and seemed like a really nice gal. When asked how she was able to lie and steal in the game, she answered ... *I was an actor in the game.*

For most of our lives, we play as actors. We have personas we play online, with our friends, at home and at work. All these different personas have their benefits. They help us pay the bills, they help us function in a job in which we struggle, and help us deal with people or clients with whom we would rather not want to deal.

Often we are so busy maintaining our different personas that we lose sight of who we are. We then try to live up to what others think of us at the expense of ourselves. This is not a conscious decision, and many times we find ourselves waking up to this reality later on.

I have a friend of a friend ... I've never had the privilege of meeting him, yet he's still managed to make his way into this book. His heart is just that big. I haven't met him yet, because he's spent the last 24 years in prison. He was given a 30-year sentence for cooking meth. When I look at a picture of him, I might just notice a big, tough man with tattoos and prison clothes. That might be all that many people see. But God saw so much more...

One day Mike walked into a kitchen at the city jail and stumbled upon a group of gangsters gathered around. They weren't dealing in anything Mike had been used to up to the point—no drugs here. Instead, these men were "dealing out the Word of God". It was a Bible study. As Mike listened in, several childhood verses he remembered came alive to him for the first time. That was 1996. Ever since that day, Mike has dedicated his time in prison to ministering to others. As my close friend (also a convicted felon) has said, "Mike was the guy I wanted to be like when I was locked away. I'd send everyone with questions about Jesus over to him. He'd know how to explain things and he'd know how to reach them."

Now, Mike has used his ministry skills within the form of a children's story called *The Little Peach Tree*. There's something about that name that just makes me smile, thinking of big, strong, tattooed Mike sitting down in his cell to write about a little peach tree. It has yet to be published (I hope someday it will be), but Mike has graciously granted permission to give a summary of his story here.

The setting of the story goes like this: there is a great, wide forest full of beautiful oak trees. It was a cherished place to the townspeople, who would come with their families to picnic, especially under Grandpa Oak, the biggest and wisest of all the trees. One day, a young boy came to sit under the big oak, cheeks wet with tears because of the constant bullying he had to face. He ate his lunch under that tree, feeling comforted, and tossed the peach seed he'd eaten around onto the ground by the big oak. In essence, the little peach tree was birthed with tears.

In the years ahead, the little peach tree may also have had reason to cry. For many years, he went unnoticed, too small for his voice to be heard. When he finally got the attention of the larger oaks, they only made fun of him. Why was this little peach tree allowed to be in such a grand oak forest? No other trees wanted to give him any sun, none except Grandpa Oak. The biggest and wisest oak never spoke against the little peach tree, and he would move his branches so as to shine the light on him.

Many years later, it was time to harvest the oak forest. The young boy who had planted the peach seed in tears was now a man, and he happened to work for the lumber company. He recognized the little peach tree by Grandpa Oak, and couldn't bear to cut them down. Instead, the two trees remained, a gathering place for families to enjoy the shade of the oak and the fresh peaches. All the newly planted oak trees looked up at the little peach tree and would say they wanted to be like him. But Grandpa Oak knew better. The story ends with Grandpa Oak looking down at the new trees and comforting them, "It's better to be just who you are, little ones. It's better to be just who you are."

When I look at Mike's acknowledgements, it brings tears to my eyes. He writes, "I want to take this time to thank the Lord Jesus, because He saw what was in me when the world and everyone else did not, even myself. I thank Him for the love He gave to me, and for teaching me how to love myself and others ... I want [you] to know that even though you cannot see the sun, it is always shining. It is better to be who you are, and always look at the bright side of things ... Everybody has a chance to change." - Michael Schutte.

It's interesting to me that positive change can't really happen until you learn to accept yourself for who you are. When you embrace the truth that you are beautifully designed by God to be you .. that is when you can finally grow into the best version of yourself. All the acting and the personas and the self-defeating thoughts are only shielding you from seeing the sunlight.

"Know thyself" is an old Latin saying[2]. To know thyself requires self-awareness, a conscious examination of thoughts, intentions, emotions, actions, and patterns. When you are aware of the things you do that are detrimental to you, you can stop. It all starts with your thoughts, which lead to your emotions, which will then lead to your behavior.

Did you know that butterflies remember their days as a caterpillar[3]? It was always the same creature, just different stages, and the butterfly is not ashamed of its humble beginnings. To know thyself, or to examine oneself, must leave room for a change of self. Do not fall into the trap of becoming so aware of negative patterns in your life that you begin to identify with those attributes. André Gide wrote in *Autumn Leaves* (1950): 'A caterpillar who seeks to know himself would never become a butterfly.' Keep in mind that part of who you are is someone with the ability to transform. You hold the power of that transformation. That power is in your mind.

Question:

1. Are you staying true to your design? How can you use this 'design' to accomplish more in life?

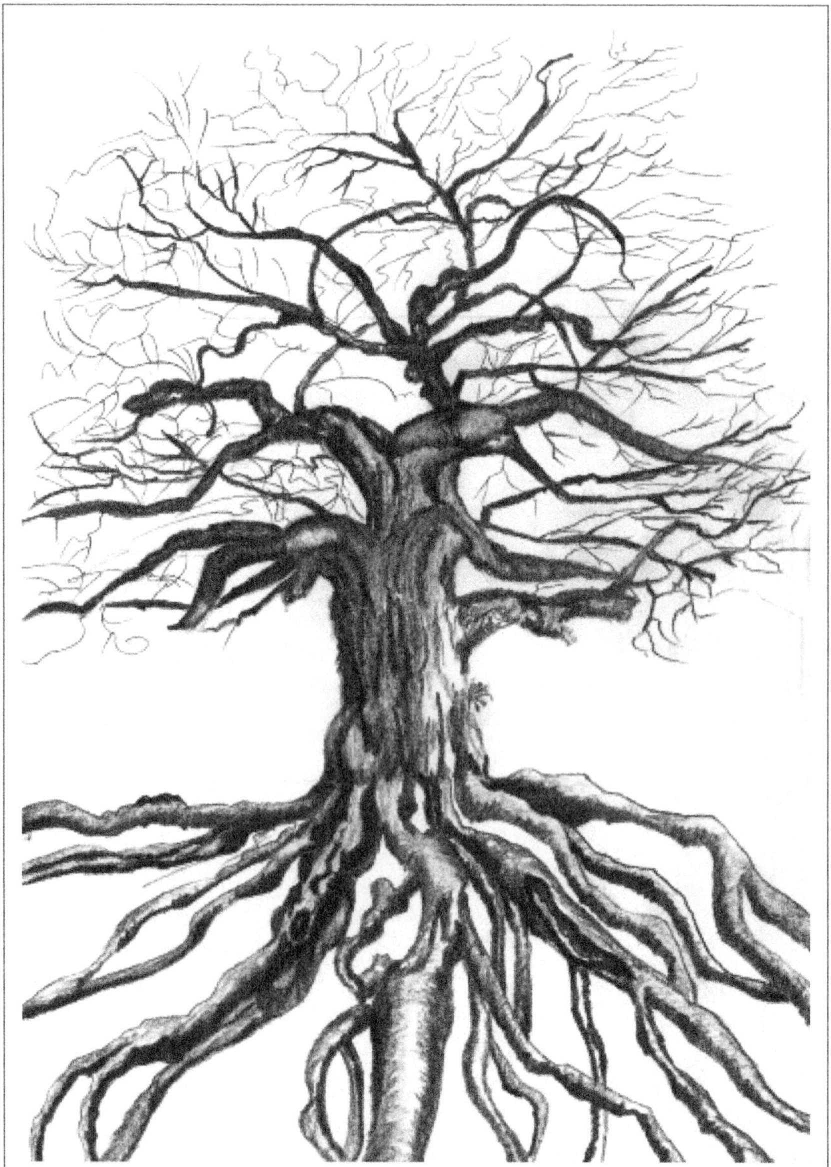

CHAPTER 3

Body, Soul, and Spirit Connection

"Now may the God of peace Himself sanctify you completely; and may your whole spirit, soul, and body be preserved blameless at the coming of our Lord Jesus Christ."

(1 Thessalonians 5:23)

Before we focus our attention on the mind, I want to cover how intricately designed we are, that no one part of us stands isolated. We are not simply a body, and not simply a soul, nor simply a spirit. When we have a better understanding of this, we'll be able to better harness the power of our minds to draw upon each of these parts, as well as train aspects of these in order to create a healthier state of being.

In 1 Thessalonians 5:23, Paul speaks of us being a 3-part system of body, soul and spirit. With our bodily senses we can smell, taste, see, hear, feel. What about the spiritual? Scripture is full of examples where individuals would see, eat, and taste in the spirit. Think about the book of Ezekiel. Ezekiel 3:1 states, "And he said to me, 'Son of man, eat what is before you, eat this scroll; then go and speak to the house of Israel.'" Evidently, Ezekiel used his senses while in the spirit.

Since this is experienced in the Spirit, what can we say about all of this? It seems like we don't have only five senses, but more like ten! Each of these senses are working to find our connection and mode of interaction with our surroundings. And what about the soul? How does our soul play into this complex sensory network which influences not only our responses, but our state of being?

Let's imagine that you and I walk down the road and a huge dog runs toward us. We visually see the dog with our physical senses, and it is then internally processed through our mental filters, one of our mental filters being our past.

For me, I have no problem with big dogs; I grew up with them. My reaction would be to stand still and try to call him closer in order to see if he has a collar. After a quick observation of the dog, I may see that he has a collar with a name tag, so I'd start petting him in an attempt to get him to quiet down, that way I can see the owner's number to call, if necessary.

You, on the other hand, might have been bitten by a big dog when you were three years old, and are petrified when you see him. You may scream in panic. You may either freeze in place, begin crying, or start running in an attempt to get away from the dog. Maybe, in that moment, you remembered the smell of the dog who bit you years ago.

So are our senses limited to the five physical ones we've been taught? It's the same dog, but your perception (the "sense" you got) of the dog changed your emotion, which in turn changed your behavior. Our "state of being" is a conglomeration of information from our physical senses, our spiritual senses, as well as from our soul. Yes, our soul "senses". Some Jews believe the soul's part to play in this is something so deep that it's in your very organs.

As if adding our spiritual and soul senses wasn't enough, let me expand upon the body senses—beyond the hear, see, smell, taste, touch—your body itself carries memory of past events. Ever heard of muscle memory? It's kind of like that, but more.

Here's an interesting story:

An eight-year-old girl, who received the heart of a murdered ten-year-old girl, began having recurring vivid nightmares about the murder. Her mother arranged a consultation with a psychiatrist who after several sessions concluded that she was witnessing actual physical incidents[1].

They decided to call the police, who then used the detailed descriptions of the murder (the time, the weapon, the place, the clothes he wore, what the little girl he killed had said to him) given by the little girl to find and convict the man in question. Wow! Notice, this information did not come from the typical five physical senses; it came from memory stored within a part of the body itself.

To treat my clients as a whole, I take into account the human complexity—body, soul, and spirit. Although this book will mainly focus on mental health and its effects on the body, I want to share a testimony of a client in which her body was affecting her mind. I hope it further illustrates the connection between each part of us.

Amy is a beautiful teenager who is diagnosed with Bipolar and suffers from depression and anxiety. She does self-harm, and says that is the only way she can 'let go". She would get physically sick many times, and she was always tired. I did not understand what to do. She was seeing a psychiatrist and was on medication, but her body still suffered.

"When I walk, I see my feet, but it doesn't feel like my feet. I don't think it's a part of my body. My body feels as though it is a flesh suit ... something that does not belong to me. My body is a prison which I cannot get out of," Amy confided in me.

It made me wonder ... what if the scientists are right? According to medical research, "Trauma symptoms are not caused by the external event. They develop when excessive energy is not discharged from the body."[2] Have you ever witnessed when an antelope is chased by a predator, and the chase is unsuccessful? What is the first thing the antelope will do? He will shake himself in order to get rid of excessive energy. Shaking is the natural way to release tension and return the body to its normal homeostasis. It is a primal impulse to a stressful situation.

Maybe shaking is what we are supposed to do, but we are taught to take it, smile, hold back our tears, and "just be brave". Sadly this demeanor will trap stress in our bodies, and it will affect every part of our being. When something traumatic happens to us, we bottle it up inside, and because we are not wired like that, we 'self destruct'. Animals seem to be able to dissipate stress, but we, on the other hand, have lost our ability to recalibrate our nervous system. When we sense a threat, the body releases huge amounts of stress hormones to help us overcome the danger. This is commonly known as the flight-fight response. It kicks in, and we literally shake with fear.

I've started doing Integrated Body Therapy, a hands-on technique involving physical exercises to release trauma. I used this therapy with Amy and now she is a new person. She no longer has the urge to hurt herself, because the culprit (the body in this case) started to heal.

Just like a virus on a computer, so will unprocessed trauma create havoc in your body. It will cause your mental and physical processes to malfunction and go haywire. Whether we want to believe it or not, it's not just the brain which holds onto our trauma, our body's cells leave an imprint of a traumatic event, also.

So here is a challenge for you: whenever you are triggered by something or someone, I want you to ask yourself *why* it triggers you. Let the scenario play over in your head until you make sense of things in your life and the responses you've developed because of prior experiences. This is a new beginning for you.

With this understanding of how each part of us is connected, we can take a broad look at how everything is filtered through our mind. Any unresolved issues and memories will be in the trees ... swaying in the wind. In the next chapter, we'll tap into exactly how our mind works and how we can prune away some of those unwanted branches.

Question:

Do you know that God accepts every part of you?

Even the pieces you try to hide?

Do you sometimes feel as if your whole being is not completely integrated—Spirit, Soul, and Body?

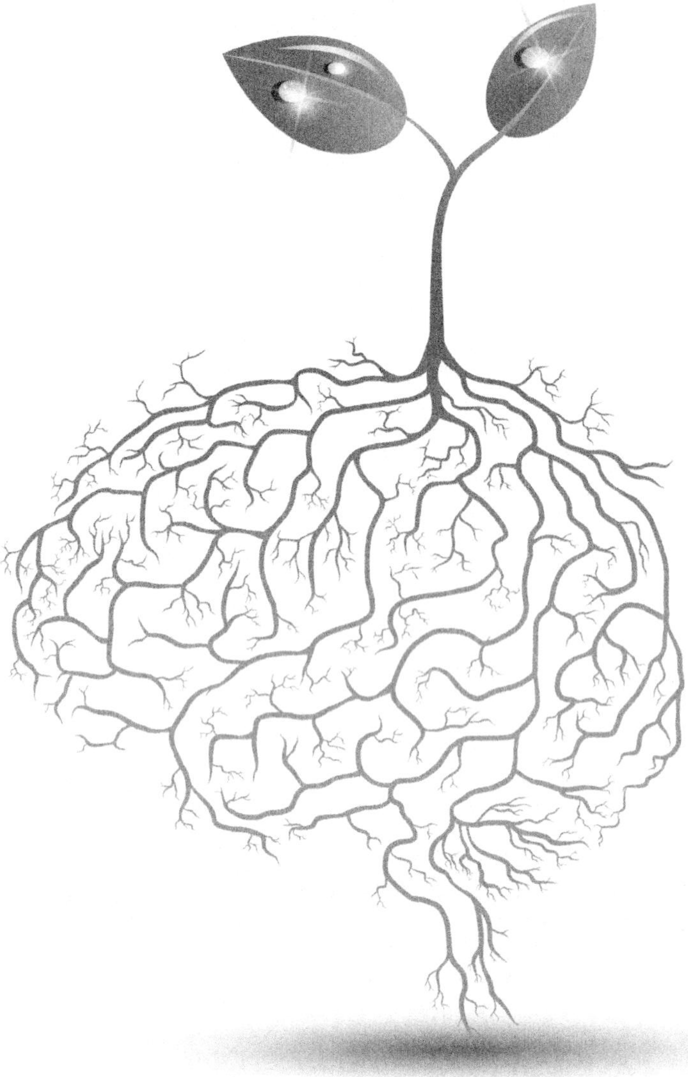

CHAPTER 4

The Cognitive Model:

TAPPING INTO OUR BRAIN TREES

"No matter how tall or wide a tree is, it started off a seed."

Matshona Dhliwayo

Many people I've counseled have come to me with only a thread of hope left. Having significant change in their lives seemed near impossible. Others come expecting a quick fix. The good news is that change is always possible, but some changes take time to grow and establish. Part of that process is becoming more aware of things.

Cognitive Behavioral Therapy (CBT) has become one of the leading approaches to psychotherapy due to its strong research support and quick treatment timeline. Once you learn how CBT works, you will find that it can easily be applied to your life. It just makes sense. For you to be able to use CBT effectively, you first need to have a strong understanding of the cognitive model.

Situation (interpreted) → Thought → Emotion → Behavior

CBT is a form of psychotherapy which assumes that unproductive or unhelpful thinking causes undesired negative emotions and thus unproductive behavior. Emotions don't come out of nowhere; they don't stand isolated. Emotions are responses to our thoughts.

Thoughts, emotions, and behaviors are all interlinked. Your interpretation of the situation will give rise to certain thoughts, which will give way to an emotion and, lastly, it will result in you acting a certain way. So how do you interpret everyday life?

CBT is solution-focused in helping people to help themselves. We possess the ability to regulate ourselves, yet if you are not aware of yourself, then you cannot self-regulate. Let me explain it in a bit more detail. Many crimes are committed by individuals thinking that they are their thoughts. However, your thought is just a thought—it has no power over you. You give it the power if you act upon that thought. You either choose A or B. Why are the prisons full? They are full because people do not self-regulate. By becoming aware of yourself, your weaknesses, your strengths, and your faults, you will begin understanding yourself.

Every person is solely responsible for their own happiness, it is not dependent upon anyone else, or on an outside source, but on you. I've found that when people begin taking responsibility for themselves, it diminishes all victim mentality. If we all self-regulate and take responsibility for our own happiness, how would the world change?

We cannot control how people feel about us or what they think of us. What we can decide is how to act upon it. When your self-value is low, anything can make you irritable or angry. When self-value is high, the insults and frustrations of life just roll off your back. Think about it.

What I'm about to share with you throughout this book is not completely CBT. Rather, it is a process I'd like to call *'The Power of a Sound Mind.'* You have "not [been] given a spirit of fear, but of power and of love and of a sound mind" (2 Timothy 1:7). A sound mind, meaning that state of a man's mind which is able to reason and comes to a judgment upon ordinary subjects. In other words, your thought life can be clear of the negative voices putting you down and clouding your judgment, discouraging you, and adding confusion; a thought life free from emotions wholly determining your decisions. A sound mind ... sounds good, doesn't it?

Intervention studies have found that integrating religious clients' spiritual and religious beliefs in therapy is at least as effective in reducing depression than secular treatments. A review of 46 spiritual intervention studies concluded that patients with spiritual beliefs in spiritually integrated psychotherapies showed greater improvement than patients treated with other psychotherapies. When compared with the same type of therapy in secular form, spiritually integrated therapies showed greater improvement on spiritual outcomes and similar improvement on psychological outcomes.[1] CBT teaches individuals to identify, challenge, and replace maladaptive thoughts and distorted thinking styles with healthy thoughts and behaviors.

I want you to remember back to the previous chapter and the complexity of how we're created. We are body, soul, and spirit, and each of these parts is providing information for us to process.

When information flows from your external world to your internal world, it comes in as light waves, converted into an electric current which travels to the area in your brain that controls free will—this happens somewhere in the frontal cortex. When a thought comes into your mind and you take it captive, as the Word says, and you don't dwell on it, it will not influence your thoughts any further.

On the other hand, when you begin meditating on that person you don't like, or you start resenting your partner for something they did—and you don't take it captive—it begins growing like a cancer. A stronghold, indeed. The branches on those trees will grow, and a memory will be built into your brain.

Let's look at fear. If you have been living with fear for a prolonged period of time, your body might be producing the stress hormones as if you are in a life-or-death situation. After a prolonged period, your body will go into autopilot and put you into a state that produces the stress hormones regularly, without it even being triggered.

Someone may say to me:

"Amelia, I had a panic attack!"

"Ok, so what happened? What triggered your panic? What did you see, what do you remember?"

"Nothing happened! I was simply washing the dishes when I felt complete fear creep up, and I started going into that black hole of fear."

In this situation, the person's body has been in a state of survival for so long that it simply releases those chemicals which induce panic whether the circumstances triggered it or not.

So, you see it all starts with your thoughts…

> Who told you to be fearful?
>
> Who told you to be anxious?
>
> Who told you that you are not good enough?
>
> Who told you that you are alone and separated?
>
> … I know God didn't.

We are told "do not fear" 365 times in the Bible. Philippians 4:6 tells us to "not be anxious about anything." *Anything.* So what happens when a thought arises which causes fear and anxiety? Romans 8:31 instructs us this way: "What then shall we say to these things? If God is for us, who can be against us?" Instead of allowing thoughts of God being against you to run amuck in your head, or that you are alone in this world, choose rather to think on this truth from Joshua 1:5: "as I was with Moses, so I will be with you. I will not leave you nor forsake you."

I'll say it again: if you want to be better equipped in handling life and the chaos that comes with it, you will need to self-regulate. When you realize a thought is just a thought, until you make it your own by acting upon it, it gives you a great amount of power. When you take all thoughts captive that go against the knowledge of God—in other words, discern the lies—then you will be able to lead a much healthier, happier life.

JOURNALING

So how do we get to know ourselves? I'm going to give you the first tool.

Writing can be a powerful therapeutic tool to help us examine our feelings, change our behavior, and even heal our emotional wounds. By learning to use a "thought log", a person can write about any negative situations, thoughts, and feelings. Once these items are written in a journal, a person can then examine why they feel as they do and where in their history they might have first felt that way. This helps identify patterns of thought and behavior. A "Thought Log" can also be used to create alternative responses to stressful situations and feelings that are more positive and self-affirming.

You have around 60,000 thoughts a day. Your brain will save energy by creating shortcuts. You don't think of how to tie your shoes, nor do you think of how to turn on the light. You know how to do it, so you automatically do it. All the information you take in will go through a processing system, much like a water filter. It will run through your mental filters, and will either be deleted, distorted or generalized. These mental filters are made up of things like your past, your fears, your biases and your phobias. Because we are all so unique, our experiences of the information taken in will differ.

What if your brain has made a shortcut that is detrimental to you? The way you feel about yourself, or the judgment you give to others? You have been doing it for so long, you probably don't even know you are doing it. These are called Negative Automatic Thoughts. These NAT's need to be pruned away, as they will crowd the space in your brain.

Here's the good news: you can start pruning them by becoming aware of them, controlling them, catching them, challenging them, and then changing them. Writing changes the way you view things. It's a brain trainer. During times of distress, of sadness or turmoil, writing can lift your mood and ease your depressive state. It can even recalibrate the part of the brain that has a firm grip on happy thoughts by teaching it that you are in control.

Journaling can capture your negative emotions on paper, then you can look at it at a later time when your emotions are not so fired up. This later reflection can help you get to the root of the problem. From here you can formulate ways to improve that particular negative situation.

Once you start writing it down, you can then list ways to improve your situation for the better. It will instill hope for the future. There are ways to overcome these unhappy thoughts, and you have the solution. Moving those solutions out of your head and onto paper is a major catalyst for change. I would suggest the following to clients: Start your journaling with the negative thought, but follow up with the solution. An example: Ann had a terrible day at work and feels like she should resign. "I had such a terrible day at work today, and I can't handle the stress anymore, but I know this will also pass and tomorrow is a new day for me. Let me think of ways to destress..."

Once you've gained self-awareness regarding the genesis of those negative thoughts, you can start with an action plan on how to better equip yourself for positive change.

POSITIVITY JOURNAL

Every day brings a combination of good and bad experiences. Unfortunately, the human mind tends to focus on the bad experiences. We remember fights and awkward situations more clearly than hundreds of normal interactions. Make it a point to remember positive experiences, no matter how small they are. I make it a point to remind my clients about all the small victories, every hill they climbed, and every obstacle they cleared.

Journaling is not only beneficial for writing down our negative thoughts, but also for the positive effect it has on our wellbeing. Research tells us that frequent journaling can have positive effects on our mood. I want you to look at the positivity journal. Each day, you will be asked to write three brief entries, as short as one sentence each. Each entry should describe something positive that happened. These do not have to be groundbreaking; it might be as simple as having a good dinner, or going for a relaxing walk. When you start looking deeper into what you should be grateful for, you will start looking deeper into life itself.

At the end of the day, I want you to record three things that had a positive effect on you that day, the things you are grateful for.

Monday:

Tuesday:

Wednesday:

Thursday:

Friday:

Saturday:

Sunday:

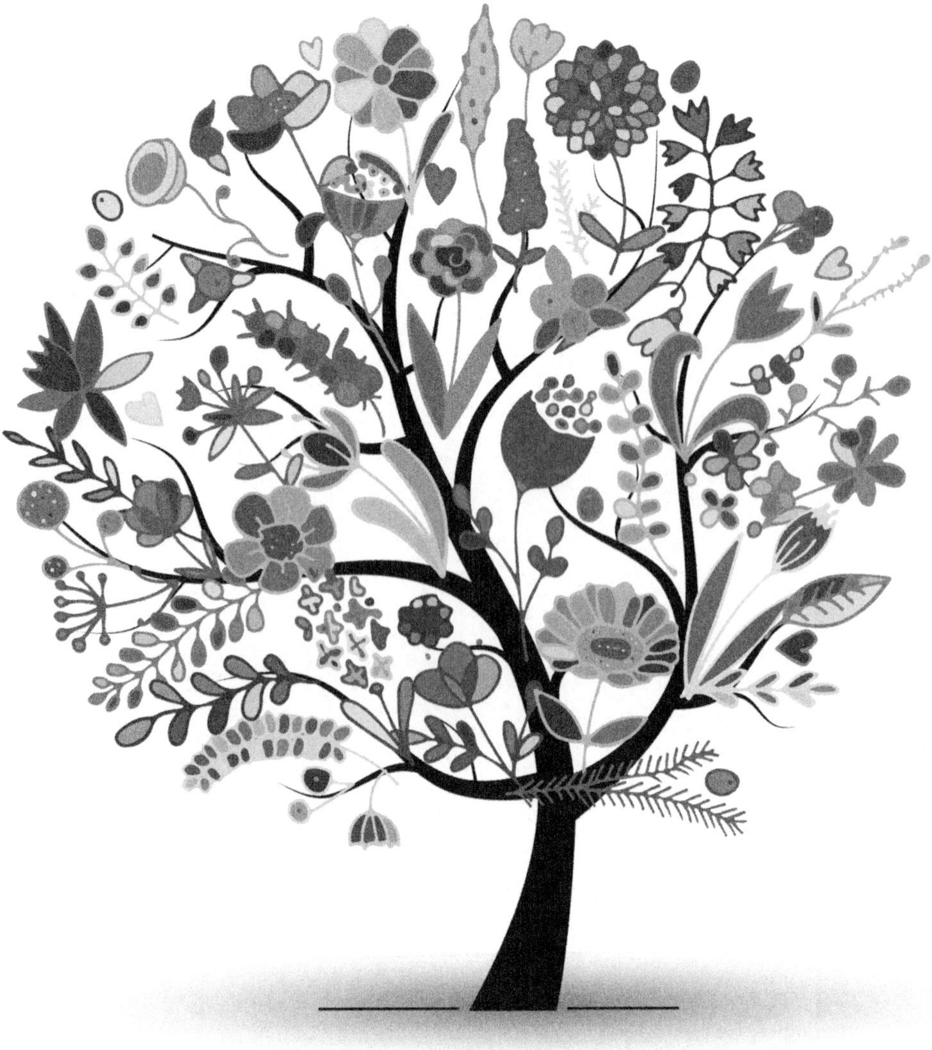

CHAPTER 5

Renewing of the Mind

"Do not conform any longer to the pattern of this world, but be transformed by the renewing of your mind. Then you will be able to test and approve what God's will is—his good, pleasing and perfect will."

(Romans 12:2)

Your brain has an amazing ability to learn, grow, and heal. In the medical world they call it re-transcribing the mind, or neuroplasticity. We simply call it 'Renewing of the Mind.' Renewed thinking is where spiritual transformation takes place. I've seen this happen over and over again. A client will have a certain thought or memory that will just not go away. Through renewing the mind and taking thoughts captive that go against the knowledge of God, you can find healing for your mind.

I'll use an example:

Roger had a terrible argument with his in-laws in the past. Every time he would see them after the incident, he would be reminded of the event, reliving it, playing it over and over in his head. Over a period of time, Roger's brain had grown accustomed to the stress hormones released, even though the event had passed. Eventually, the consistent release of these stress hormones began taking its toll on his body, making him physically sick—all from his own thoughts.

If Roger were to forgive his in-laws and deal with his emotions of anger and resentment, his brain would build new, healthy memories over those toxic thoughts. This is referred to as renewing your mind. I believe the good Lord gave us instructions like 'forgive others', because He is the designer of our bodies and knows what happens internally if we don't.

If you've worked through journaling, you may have recognized the source of your anger, frustration, or self defeating behavior. Given that my behavior begins in my mind, and my mind is where spiritual transformation takes place, this is really where you need to be strong and stand on what you believe. You will often see how people try and change on the outside. They will change what they wear or change their activities. All this change may be for the better. However, if you have not changed from the inside, it probably won't last. Remember how Jesus spoke to the Pharisees? "Woe to you, scribes and Pharisees, hypocrites! For you cleanse the outside of the cup and dish, but inside they are full of extortion and self-indulgence" (Matthew 23:25). Whatever is on the inside will make its way to the outside.

CBT teaches individuals to identify, challenge, and replace maladaptive thoughts and distorted thinking styles with healthy thoughts and behaviors. What does your stream of consciousness, or "inside conversation", sound like? There are words floating through our minds at all times; some are good and purposeful, and others are not. Thoughts are either generalized, distorted, or deleted. Most people I meet have a distorted sense of self as well as a distorted view of God and others. It's time to renew your mind!

So how do we change our thinking?

MINDFULNESS

"Be still and know that I am God."

(Psalm 46:10)

It can be easy to throw out terms like "renewing your mind", but how does one do it? It can feel like an impossible challenge, but it doesn't have to be. One simple way to begin the process of renewing your mind is through *mindfulness*.

Many attribute mindfulness to eastern spirituality and are thus cautious of anything that could open them up to influence outside of Christ. However, there is nothing inherently dangerous about mindfulness. The point is simply in the intentional directing of one's mind. It's origin was with God and not in any religious practice of which we need be wary.

This concept can be found throughout scripture. Proverbs 7:1-3 instructs us to "keep my words, and treasure my commands within you. Keep my commands and live, and my law as the apple of your eye. Bind them on your fingers; write them on the tablet of your heart." Simply put, be ever-mindful of these teachings until they become a part of you!

Philippians 4:8 similarly instructs us, "Finally, brethren, whatever things are true, whatever things are noble, whatever things are just, whatever things are pure, whatever things are lovely, whatever things are of good report, if there is any virtue and if there is anything praiseworthy—meditate on these things." Other versions of this verse tell us to *dwell* on these things. This verse is significant in that it instructs us to be mindful not only concerning teachings or commands, it expands the focus to the good and pure and beautiful things in life for which we can be grateful and respond in joy to the goodness of God. In other words, I'm not asking you to just go memorize scripture as if it were a religious assignment. Mindfulness is about changing how we *perceive* and, in turn, changing how we *respond* to the world in our everyday lives.

Here's a simple exercise in mindfulness: Let's say you are eating a sandwich—a tomato and lettuce sandwich. I want you to look at the sandwich without eating it. I mean *really* look at it. Don't eat it. Just look at it. You've probably seen thousands of sandwiches, but you've never seen this specific one at this specific time in your current state of mind. Look at this sandwich like it's the first one you've ever seen. Look at the colors in the sandwich. Look at the tomato ... that tomato that was grown somewhere in rich, fertile soil, where someone tended to its nourishment until it was time to carefully harvest it. The lettuce, also, was cared for, harvested and became a means of provision for someone and their family. Think about the Creator who made the sun shine on the lettuce and tomato and who made it all possible. He called the clouds and He brought rain to the land. Take the sandwich in your hand and feel the texture of the bread. Use all your senses and explore the sandwich. Eat the sandwich with great gratitude to the One who made it all possible.

An important aspect of mindfulness is simply being *still* for the moment. As the above Psalm stated, be still before God, and you'll find peace for your mind, heart, and spirit. Mindfulness puts emphasis on being present in the moment and not dwelling on thoughts about the past or the future.

Be grateful. Every time you are mindful of being grateful, you are building and strengthening a neural pathway of gratitude. The more that pathway of gratitude is traveled, the more familiar it becomes. The more familiar it becomes, the more your brain programs itself to release healthy hormones as opposed to toxic ones. Such is the power of mindfulness.

REPLACE SELF-FOCUSED THINKING WITH A GOD-FOCUSED MINDSET.

Metanoia. I've always loved this word; it has such a deep meaning. Metanoia is the Greek word for repentance. It means a total mind shift, completely shifting the way one thinks. That means that if you were walking to the right, you would turn around and walk to the left. If what you have been doing in the past has not been working, then set your mind on a new beginning, a God-focused mindset.

Jesus was constantly introducing a shift in thinking to his disciples.

At one point, Jesus told the disciples what would happen to Him. This idea obviously didn't sit right with Peter, who decided to take Jesus aside and rebuke Him. (C'mon ... who rebukes God??) Something very significant is revealed in this process, however. Let's see how Jesus handled Peter's rebuke: "Peter took Him aside and began to rebuke Him. 'Far be it from You, Lord!' he said. 'This shall never happen to You!' But He turned and said to Peter, 'Get behind Me, Satan! *You are an offense to Me, for you are not mindful of the things of God, but the things of men*" (Matthew 16:23).

What was the offense? The offense was to not have in mind the things of God, but the things of men. God's plan before creation was for Jesus to make His temple in us. We were predestined to be adopted and share the relationship inside of the Trinity. Peter obviously wanted Jesus to stay with them. However, in trying to stop Jesus from dying, this would ultimately prevent us from becoming the temple. Thus, Peter did not have the things of God in mind, but the things of men. Peter needed to shift his way of thinking to the things of God.

To focus my mind on God requires some work. If I don't take purposeful action to *set my mind on Jesus Christ*, then I'm allowing my mind to go anywhere it wants to go. Personally, I know where my mind will go if I'm not purposeful, and it's nowhere good. So I have the choice: will I meditate on God and His goodness, or will I allow the world to take over my mind with worries, anxiety, and stress?

SCRIPTURE MEDITATION

> "For You formed my inward parts; You covered me in my mother's womb. I will praise You, for I am fearfully and wonderfully made; marvelous are Your works, and that my soul knows very well. My frame was not hidden from You, when I was made in secret" (Psalm 139:13-15).

What is it that you stand on? What is it that you believe? Is it real? Is it something worth thinking about?

I have gone through life-threatening situations in my life where I have been so scared, I literally thought I would die. I would feel the nudging from the Holy Spirit telling me that He will never leave me nor forsake me. In the Old Testament, He goes before you and He goes behind you. He is on your left and on your right. King David once wrote, "Where can I go to hide from Your presence?" (Psalm 139:7). He knew that it doesn't matter where you go, God is there—the everlasting God, the everlasting arms. As He is maintaining and sustaining all of creation, He is then also maintaining and sustaining you. It does not matter if you get lost in yourself, He knows exactly where you are.

Faith = Truth When you get to know Him, your reality changes. When you know the truth, it shall set you free. As we live in a Christ-based reality, your reality is then *Christ*. He is the Light that shines through all the darkness. His Light is not a light that stops with a physical barrier, He shines IN the darkness.

If you are in darkness and you feel like there is no way out, walk with me through these exercises and you will renew your mind and thoughts. I want you to start memorizing different scripture. My disclaimer is that it's vitally important that you not approach this as if you're in a scripture memorization competition to see how many you can recite whereas it becomes just another expectation on you, or just another means of evaluating yourself—the world and religion has enough of that. I simply ask you to memorize the scripture so that as you're taking steps to reject the negative thoughts and emotions which arise, you have this comfort at the ready. One day it will be more than a moment-to-moment comfort, it will become a part of who you are.

The scriptures you choose to memorize will depend on where you are in life and with which area you need help. Below are a few examples.

*If you struggle with feeling alone:

> **Psalm 27:10** "When my father and my mother forsake me, then the Lord will take care of me."

1 Samuel 12:22 "For the Lord will not forsake His people, for His great name's sake, because it has pleased the Lord to make you His people."

*If you struggle with forgiving yourself:

1 Peter 5:7 "Cast all your anxieties on Him, because He cares for you."

Psalm 103:10-11 "He has not dealt with us according to our sins, nor punished us according to our iniquities."

*If you struggle with fear over finances:

Philippians 4:6-7 "Be anxious for nothing, but in everything by prayer and supplication, with thanksgiving, let your requests be made known to God; and the peace of God, which surpasses all understanding, will guard your hearts and minds through Christ Jesus."

Nahum 1:7 "The Lord is good, a stronghold in the day of trouble; and He knows those who trust in Him"

*If you struggle with reacting in anger:

James 1:19-20 "So then, my beloved brethren, let every man be swift to hear, slow to speak, slow to wrath; for the wrath of man does not produce the righteousness of God."

Proverbs 14:29 "He who is slow to wrath has great understanding, but he who is impulsive exalts folly.»

Do you remember the verse from Philippians? It's an important one! Here it is again:

"Be anxious for nothing, but in everything by prayer and supplication, with thanksgiving, let your requests be made known to God; and the peace of God, which surpasses all understanding, will guard your hearts and minds through Christ Jesus. Finally, brethren, whatever things are true, whatever things are noble, whatever things are just, whatever things are pure, whatever things are lovely, whatever things are of good report, if there is any virtue and if there is anything praiseworthy—meditate on these things. The things which you learned and received and heard and saw in me, these do, *and the God of peace will be with you*" (Philippians 4:6-9).

Let me draw your attention to that last sentence, it's extremely and awesomely important! If you do these things ... *when* you practice the Presence and concentrate on His goodness, you will better understand the God of peace, how He moves, and you will tangibly feel His Presence.

I want you to memorize a certain piece of scripture that is applicable for the season you are in. As much as you can, even if you have to set your watch for every 30 minutes, do it until that becomes a part of your DNA.

Personal Scripture Choice:

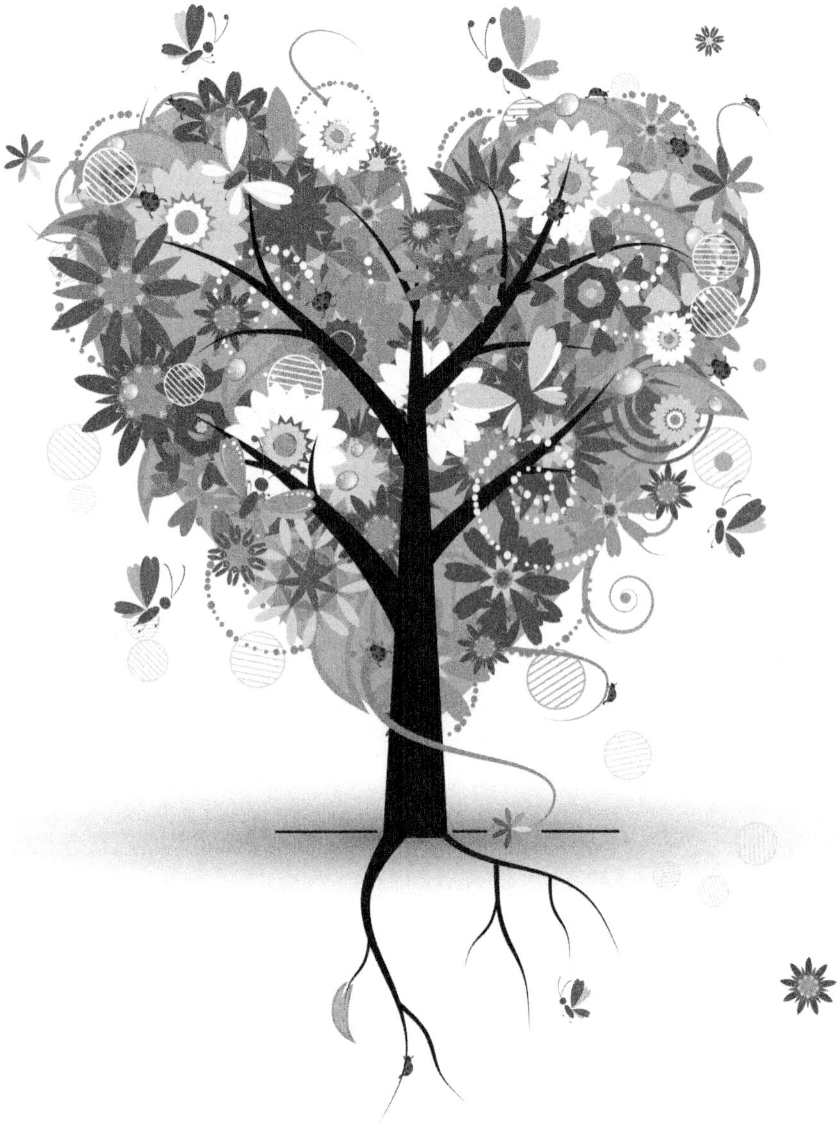

CHAPTER 6

Rest in this Truth:

YOU ARE ACCEPTED, NOT SEPARATE

"And you shall know the truth, and the truth shall make you free."
(John 8:32)

The most dangerous prisons are the ones inside of us. We all will go through trauma at some time in our life, and sometimes you want to just numb the pain. To find this "escape", some individuals will drink too much, or start using drugs, but nothing from this world can fill that hole. All of these prisons will lead to death.

You can be a prisoner of many things in life beyond drinking and drug addictions—you can be a prisoner of toxic relationships, cycles of abuse, pornography, and the list goes on. I've had clients who are prisoners of spirits of suicide, and they can't stop thinking about death. They would confide in me about how they just want to die.

There's only one kind of prisoner I want to be. Paul speaks of this when he refers to himself, "I, Paul, the prisoner of Christ Jesus" (Ephesians 3:1). Like many biblical concepts in which the spiritual application is opposite of the typical earthly application (i.e. the first will be last and the last shall be first, or whoever loses their life shall find it, etc.), when you become a "prisoner" of Jesus Christ, you become free. Being a prisoner of Jesus means that your thoughts will be consumed by Him, His goodness, and His favor in your life. With thanks and praise you will start seeing everything around you blossom with the life inside of Him.

What is ultimately holding us captive and resisting the sound mind God intended for us? After working with thousands of people, I firmly believe the ultimate crux of humanity is the inability to know how loved we are by Him. Whether I am speaking to an atheist or a Christian well-versed in all the "love" scriptures about God, the issue still boils down to the same key point ... they feel alone, separated somehow, and that they must try to *be* or *do* something to be worthy of love. Religion has done a marvelous job of wiring our brains with lots of "God loves us, *if* ..." or "God is with us, but ..." or "God forgives us, *if* ..."

Having a sound mind starts with truly hearing the sound of His voice over you. To hear Him call you by name: "I have called you by name; you are mine" (Isaiah 43:1). To hear his delight over you: "He will rejoice over you with gladness, He will quiet you with His love, He will rejoice over you with singing" (Zephaniah 3:17). To hear the sound of His call to you: "Come to Me, all you who labor and are heavy laden, and I will give you rest." (Matthew 11:28). *Come home.* Can you hear Him?

I see in my mind's eye how Jesus was pleading with those suffering under the law. I can hear Him saying, "Come all of you who are tired and who can't get it right. Come to me and I will give you rest. Don't tie your worth to the law; you won't ever get it right 100 percent."

Jesus goes on to tell His disciples that it's better if He goes away. If He does not go away, the Comforter will not come to them. Jesus was clearly doing very 'unorthodox things'—healing on the Sabbath, etc. In essence, Jesus was telling them that He needs to go in order for the Holy Spirit to make things clear to them. John 16:8-11 states, "When he comes, he will prove the world to be in the wrong about sin and righteousness and judgment: about sin, because people do not believe in me; about righteousness, because I am going to the Father, where you can see me no longer; and about judgment, because the prince of this world now stands condemned."

1. You are wrong about sin. Sin is not what you think it is. I am standing in front of you, and you are not coming to Me. That is your sin. If you would come to me, you would learn who I am and you would change. Come to me.

2. You are wrong about righteousness, because I am the One going to the Father. On your own you will never be able to make it. Come to me.

3. You are wrong about judgment, because the devil is the one judged and condemned. It's not you.

Jesus makes it clear to humanity that we are all a bit blind, and when we judge, we do it from a human standpoint with all our mental filters and distortions. He is the One with a full view on Life. The Father has left all judgment to the Son, (John 5:22) and He could judge us, but He doesn't. "You judge according to the flesh; I judge no one" (John 8:15). He is not the accuser of the brethren, *He is the Lover of the human race.*

You are completely accepted by Him and unconditionally called to be His. There are no hoops to jump through. Your eternity will not be based on religion, tradition, or works. Rather, it will be based on *relationship*. Does He know you? Have you taken the time? We will always be in His presence, it does not matter where we go. All of humanity will be in His presence, we simply make the decision on how this eternity will look. "Our God is a consuming fire" (Hebrews 12:29). The question is, are you burning like He is?

We can never be separated from Him; it is impossible. He is the one holding creation together (Colossians 1:17). If we could maintain ourselves and exist separate from Him, we would actually be "breaking the rules" of scripture at large. Self-existence would make us gods. In reality, the same Creator speaking galaxies into existence is the One holding you.

He is the very breath we breathe. Our life starts in the hands of the Father and ends in the hands of the Father. The most painful lie still marauding around the earth today, stealing our peace and joy, is that we could ever be separated from Him.

> "For I am persuaded that neither death nor life, nor angels nor principalities nor powers, nor things present nor things to come, nor height nor depth, nor any other created thing, shall be able to separate us from the love of God which is in Christ Jesus our Lord" (Romans 8:38-39).

In the beginning the Word brought everything into existence, and this same Word—the eternal Logos—became flesh. God became human, and inside of Jesus Christ humanity has been forever reconciled with Him. "That is, that God was in Christ reconciling the world to Himself" (2 Corinthians 5:19). This verse goes on to state that He has committed the message of reconciliation to us. It's sadly ironic that although many take up this commitment to spread the message, they forget to preach it to themselves. What does His voice sound like to you? The answer to that question is key to having a sound mind. The message of reconciliation is a message saying **you** have been reconciled! Now live like it!

THE LIGHT THAT SHINES IN THE DARKNESS

Christ is the Eternal Light, shining through all of creation, never stopping. It is unlike created light that stops when there is a physical barrier. This is an ever-existing Light that has been there since the beginning, and it shines on you, your family, your neighbor, even your enemy. It shines through galaxies of which we are not even aware, and it shines in a microorganism. The very

Light of creation is the glue keeping everything together. Let me assure you—this Light is a person, not a force.

The Light shines in the darkness and darkness does not understand it, comprehend it, recognize it, or overcome it.

Let's imagine, for example, that you have been lost in the wilderness for a long time. Finally, you see a house and go inside, hoping that someone is there who can help you. Upon entering, you find yourself in complete darkness, which causes you to stumble around and fall. You're tired. Thirsty. Famished.

What you don't see is that I have a very bright light on in my kitchen, but you cannot comprehend it. In other words, it's not that there is an absence of light, it's that you are blind to it. If you can't see it, nor comprehend it, then you can't participate in it. It does not change the fact that there is a light on in my kitchen. I am in my kitchen and I am calling you out of the darkness. My cupboards are loaded with food and the kettle is on for us to sit down and catch up. You are free to take whatever you want from my kitchen; I'll share whatever I have with you.

Come sit with me; there is so much more I can tell you.

When clients would compliment me on the work I do, I would always say, tongue in cheek, that I put a lot of energy into pretending to know what I am talking about! Then we all have a good laugh and we carry on with the conversation. This stuck with me. How much do we really know? According to the Center for the Study of Global Christianity, estimations show a staggering 45,000 denominations of Christianity worldwide.[1] Each one of these thinks they know something that the others don't. Everyone seems to have more knowledge than their neighbor.

I'll tell you a truth that is explicitly Truth, never changed and never will. Two thousand years ago a baby was born in Bethlehem, but it turns out this was not just any baby. The Creator who holds everything together, sustains all and maintains all, became a human being and stepped into our darkness. Yes, the One who spoke galaxies into existence and held your name in His—He was born as a baby on earth. Yet, He wasn't just a baby.

A few decades later He walked around in Israel and managed to really get under the skin of the Pharisees. He could do miracles, He knew the scriptures by heart, and He had the audacity to call God his Father. He wasn't just a prophet.

The religious establishment got tired of Him, tortured and crucified Him, but He rose from the dead. He wasn't just a man.

He was the Light that was shining in the darkness. He came to open their eyes and tell them, *The Father is good. He is really, really good.*

If we are able to take any advice about the Father from anyone, let it be from Jesus. He entered our darkness as a Light that shines, and nothing can stop Him. Throughout this book, I will talk a lot about perception and how wrong we have been in our views about God.

Let's look at the story of the prodigal son. Prior to Jesus telling this parable, He tells the people how the Father feels when one person has Metanoia. He goes on to tell of a son who demanded his inheritance from his father. That is basically like saying *I wish you were dead* in my opinion.

His broken-hearted father gave him his inheritance, and the son left, only to squander his money until he had nothing left. To get by, he started working for someone to look after their pigs, yet his hunger became so great that he wished he could just eat some of the pods that were thrown to the pigs.

And then the gospel spoke to him ... *I want to go home, I want to be in the presence of my father, I want to be able to eat!*

He packed up (and probably had some cognitive behavior therapy himself, thinking about how stupid he had been). I can imagine him thinking over and over what he would say to his father. The next verse I'll take straight from scripture... even if I wanted to, no one says it as beautifully as He does:

> "But when he was still a great way off, his father saw him and had compassion, and ran and fell on his neck and kissed him. And the son said to him, 'Father, I have sinned

> against heaven and in your sight, and am no longer worthy to be called your son.'"

Do you know what the father did?

> "But the father said to his servants, 'Bring out the best robe and put it on him, and put a ring on his hand and sandals on his feet. And bring the fatted calf here and kill it, and let us eat and be merry; for this my son was dead and is alive again; he was lost and is found.' And they began to be merry" (Luke 15:20-24).

Although the son was trying his best to repent, the father drowned out the voice of repentance. Take note, the father did not tell him that he's a wicked son who needs to repent before allowing him inside the house. What mattered to him was that his son was home. He had been lost, and then he was found. In order to lose something, it must have belonged with you. The son belongs with the father, and once found, he found his true place of belonging. He gave the son his ring, sandals, and robe as part of his identity. (Worth noting—The Father cannot be a Father without the Son, and the Son could not be the Son without the Father. It's relational. In the Old Testament He was the Father of nations, but when Jesus was born He was Abba Father, a personal Father.)

I had mentioned in the very beginning that I am not a universalist, and I would like to further explain myself. When I was a child, I wished to develop a time machine. I really wanted to walk alongside Jesus and see how He would do things. Or, what would happen if we were able to spend a few days with Paul or Peter? What about Athanasias or one of the other saints? Wouldn't it be better to hear from them who Jesus was, rather than the thousands of contrasting teachers two thousand years after him?

Saint Cyril of Alexandria was the patriarch from 412 to 444. He was enthroned when the city was at the height of its influence and power within the Roman Empire. He had a commentary on the book of John. When you read it and see how the Greeks would interpret it, it changes the framework of the whole chapter.

Below is a typical translation from our Bibles of John 1:1-5. The version I've chosen to use throughout this book is the NKJV. Here it states:

> "In the beginning was the Word, and the Word was with God, and the Word was God. He was in the beginning with God. All things were made through Him, and without Him nothing was made that was made. In Him was life, and the life was the light of men. And the light shines in the darkness, and the darkness did not comprehend it."

The Greek interpretation looks different from the English. Because the full stop is moved, the scope of the sentence will change.

Cyril of Alexandria Commentary:

> "In the Beginning was the Word.
>
> And the Word was with God
>
> And the Word was God.
>
> This was in the beginning with God
>
> All things were made by Him, and without Him was not anything made
>
> That which was made, in it was Life.
>
> And the Life was the light of men
>
> Without Him nothing was made that has been made.
>
> or
>
> without Him was not anything made.
>
> That which was made, in it was Life."[2]

What he is saying is that everything that was created by God has His light inside of it. *All* of creation ... nothing is left out.

Let's jump to Colossians 1:15-17:

> "He is the image of the invisible God, the firstborn over all creation. For by Him all things were created that are

> in heaven and that are on earth, visible and invisible,
> whether thrones or dominions or principalities or powers.
> All things were created through Him and for Him. And
> He is before all things, and in Him all things consist."

Can it be that every person born on this earth has the Light of the Creator inside of them? If that is the case, it isn't about who has the Light and who doesn't; rather, it comes down to a choice you make: will you say yes, or will you say *no* to Him?

When broken people come to see me, they tell me they have been to numerous psychologists and therapists. Most of them are operating/living from a fallen mind, where God is only happy with them if they do some kind of religious activity. They also have pieces of themselves they can't even look at, and because they are not able to look at it, they believe God cannot look at it either. Essentially, they feel separated from God. They feel as though they are not good enough to be accepted into His presence, when in reality, they can't escape His presence.

If we believe what the Bible says and that everything exists inside of Him, then there is no "outside" to God. The universe thus exists in the midst of God, and it keeps growing as He stretches the heavens. Can God create outside of Himself? Think about this.

The idea of God creating outside of Himself is mostly based on ancient Greek philosophy; it's not Christian. As He made everything—everything heavenly (spiritual) and physical (earthly)—He put His life inside of it, and that Life is the Light of Men. As He is the one maintaining and sustaining everything, His Light is then in every single person on earth. Do you think I'm pushing it? It may not be what you were taught. It may go against everything you know! Yet, John 1:9 explains, "That was the true Light which gives light to **every** man coming into the world."

1 Peter 2:9 tells us, "But you are a chosen generation, a royal priesthood, a holy nation, His own special people, that you may proclaim the praises of Him who called you out of darkness into His marvelous light." You have been called out of darkness, you have been anointed, and you have been made holy and righteous.

You have been called out of darkness. The power of the enemy is darkness; the end goal is to deceive you. In other words, darkness is deception. If the enemy can blind you, you'll be in darkness and you won't be able to see His Light. Again, it does not change the fact that the Light is shining IN the darkness, it's merely your incapacity to acknowledge it.

Who is going to minister in the darkness? Who is going to step in where we can't? Jesus Christ, the only One who has no darkness in Him. The Light of Christ still shines in the darkness, in it and through it. While Jesus is holding everything together, He steps into humanity. He goes to the deepest part of our darkness and He fixes it.

Jesus is the one holding us when we can't deal with life. While we are going through life and falling around in the dark. While we are kicking, screaming and not coping ... He holds us close to Him like a good Father does. "The eternal God is your refuge, and underneath are the everlasting arms" (Deuteronomy 33:27).

Christ is in *all*, and it's not due to your choosing. You simply woke up in this reality. Your choice is to either participate in it or not. Your choice is to be in a relationship or not. Your choice is to remain in the darkness of deception, or come into the glorious Light of the Son of God. Whatever you choose, you will be standing in front of a Person who will say to you, *I knew you* or *I never knew you*.

Jesus has called you into a relationship with Him. He wants you to share in the beautiful relationship of the Father, Son and Spirit. Those that are able to see the Light can participate in the Life of Christ. This is what we then share—the Eternal life of the Creator.

This is Eternal Life ... to *know Him*.

Question:

Within this chapter, you likely came to some revelations of who God is, and how big He really is

1. In what areas have you been wrong, or uninformed?

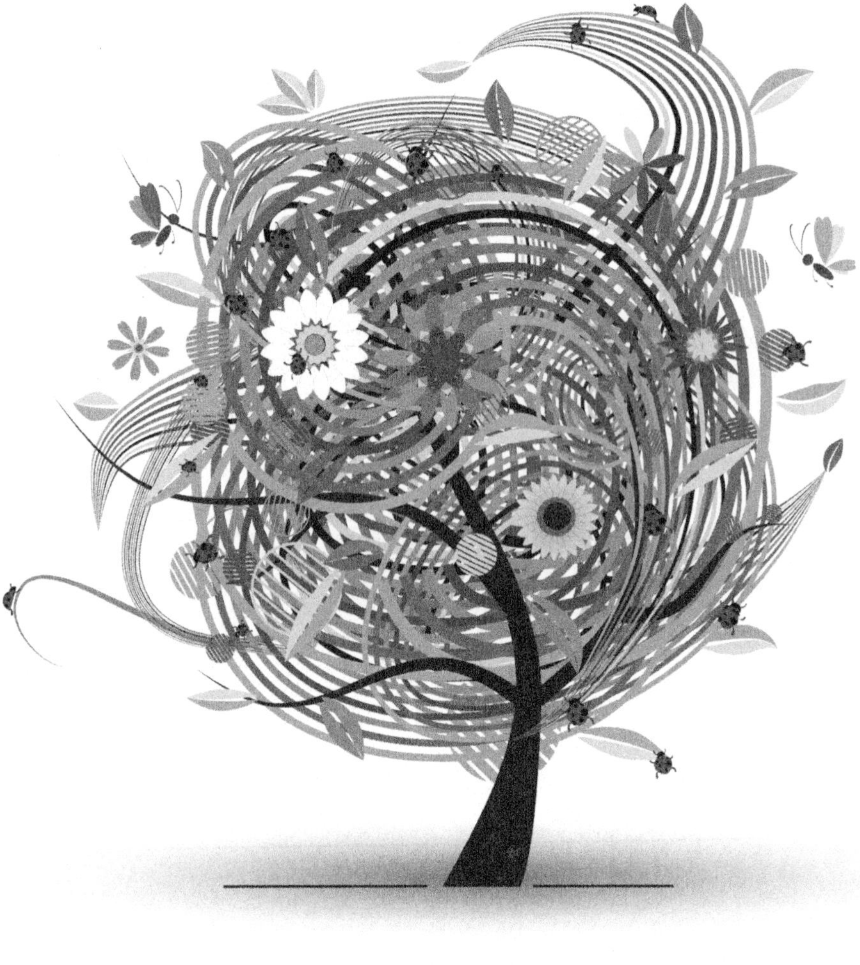

CHAPTER 7

Cognitive Distortion

"My life has been full of terrible misfortunes, most of which never happened."

Michel De Montaigne

Cognitive Distortion. My daughters are so sick and tired of me using that phrase. Whenever I hear, "I'll never be able to do this" or "Things will never change", etc., I look them in the eyes and ask them, "What are you busy with?" And they know enough to answer me: "Cognitive Distortion." (Never mind the subsequent sighs and rolling of their eyes.) I'm a proud momma.

In short, cognitive distortion is a habitual error in thinking. When you're experiencing a cognitive distortion, the way you interpret events are usually negatively biased and many times not true. Most people experience cognitive distortions from time to time. However, if the distortion is reinforced often enough, it can increase anxiety, deepen depression, cause relationship difficulties, and lead to a host of other complications.

Cognition has to do with your thought processes and your internal dialogue. When something is pulled out of shape or slanted unfavorably, it's distorted. It's like wearing strong sunglasses all day long, everywhere you go. The darkness will begin to feel like reality. After all, it's the only "reality" you know. Someone can tell you that it's not really dark outside, but if you have your glasses on, you won't realize what they are talking about ... not until you take them off.

Cognitive distortions are inaccurate thoughts that reinforce negative thought patterns or emotions. These thoughts feel natural because you are stuck in that thinking pattern for so long. They seem rational. They seem so right. You will even be able to make an *almost* airtight argument concerning it, but you may be wrong. They alter your way of looking at life and will influence you negatively for as long as you let it. A distortion is extremely toxic to you; it poisons your equilibrium.

When you are aware of what you think and alter it, you will be able to change the emotion and the corresponding undesired behavior. Here are a few of the main "textbook" cognitive distortions influencing mental health:

Negative Filtering: This is when a person is focusing on the negative, and not seeing the positive. Sometimes a single negative situation would far outweigh an abundance of positive things.

Black and White Thinking: Known as all or nothing thinking, it won't leave any room for grey. If you are not able to perform in a certain area, you might see yourself as a total failure. Many people who have this thinking pattern find it hard to have empathy for others who find themselves in toxic situations.

Catastrophizing: This is when you always assume the worst. I've found this very common, especially in people who self-confess to be perfectionists. What will help this distortion is to think about what the most desirable outcome could be, as well as what the most probable is.

Blaming: When something doesn't go the way you want it to, it's easier to put the blame on someone else. Blaming others for the way you act and feel is a cognitive distortion—that's the hard truth. You alone are responsible for the way you act and feel. Take sole responsibility to self-regulate. Be aware of how you feel and how you act.

Jumping to Conclusions: Making assumptions based on little evidence, or not having the full picture.

Emotional Reasoning: I feel it, therefore it must be true. It's worth noting here that we are called to walk by faith and not by sight ... and not by every whim of our emotions.

Always Being Right: We enjoy being right, and that's normal. Nonetheless, you are not *always* right, and assuming that others are always wrong is a cognitive distortion. When being right is consistently more important than valuing the feelings of others, you may have to rethink why you are doing it in the first place.

Shoulds: When you hold tight to personal rules of behavior, judging yourself, and others. This distortion also leaves a trail of "should-haves" in your mind.

Labeling: This is when you overgeneralize things by putting labels on people. As humans, we stand and look at people from the outside. We don't have the full picture, we only see a small part of it.

Personalization: Thinking that you are to blame for all the bad turn of events in your life. This will lead to deep feelings of insecurity.

Now that the various distortions have been identified, how do they apply? Let's take a specific circumstance and see the different reactions of several cognitive distortions.

In the New Testament, there was a certain woman brought before Jesus (see John 8). She was caught in the act of adultery, and the Pharisees wanted to stone her. If you can think about this, what cognitive distortion could the Pharisees have used to judge the situation?

1. **Filtering:** She was caught and needs to be judged. The law had to be upheld.

2. **Black and White thinking**: According to the law, she needed to die. They did not have any empathy for her, they did not know what happened in her life. Maybe she was looking for love, maybe she was lonely, maybe she was projecting, but any situational explanations were of no concern to them.

3. **Always being right**: We are right. She is wrong. We know the law and this is what it states.

4. **Labeling**: She is a 'loose woman'.

On the other hand, Jesus looked at her and did not fall into labeling or wanting to show that He was right, nor did He demand judgment. Rather, He looked at her and saw His daughter. He created her. Yes, He could judge her, but He didn't. He told her to sin no more, but had grace and love towards her. Jesus would always deal in love and relationship first, and then morality.

THE BRAIN, THE THOROUGHBRED, AND THE PONY

My very first horse was a Thoroughbred. For those not into horse lingo—a racehorse. I loved him dearly, and we would be together almost every day. We would ride, even when it was raining and it always felt like he could move at the speed of light without me doing much work. I tamed the Thoroughbred through being kind and gentle to him, but also by being stern when I needed to be.

Now, twenty years later, I am trying to teach my daughter how to ride. Unfortunately, she does not seem to get the phrase "practice makes perfect" and she wants to be able to do shows before she is able to ride properly. She has a very sweet pony that we all adore, but he just won't be hurried by her. To put it bluntly, he moves like a sloth. It doesn't matter what she does, he will stop to eat whenever he wants.

After I'd had enough of her tantrums, I told her to get off the pony. I adjusted the stirrups and got onto her pony. As soon as I got on, he was alert and ready for action. I did not raise my voice, I barely moved my hands. We went from trotting to cantering to halting. The difference was simply by the way I was sitting and how I would take control—he understood what I needed from him.

Once he came to a halt, I got off and then told my daughter that there was nothing wrong with her pony. She simply did not let him know that she was in control, and that is why he would only do what he wanted.

When I had ridden him, there was no effort on my part. It was through years of riding a Thoroughbred that I understood how their minds work and how I could use certain tools to get the pony to do what I wanted him to do, even though he was not in the mood. Your brain is like the pony. Be kind to it, but be stern. Don't let it control you!

Your brain is not your mind. Your mind is not your brain. Your mind controls your brain, and you have the mind of Christ. Have you ever wondered why some are able to walk in the supernatural? Why can some perform miracles and just flow in it? It's because they know that they have the mind of Christ and they don't need to bow down to the rules of the natural world.

You have the mind of Christ. Use it.

"For 'who has known the mind of the Lord that he may instruct Him?' *But we have the mind of Christ*" (1 Corinthians 2:16).

CHALLENGING THOUGHTS

Whenever I'm with a client, I sit down and listen to them talk. I ask them why they want to see me and with what it is they need help. After years of doing this, I realize every person has some kind of cognitive distortion through which they see the world. This is not just something you can start talking about with clients (distorted thinking), so I wait and, like a bloodhound, I sniff out irrational thoughts. I continue asking questions regarding these thoughts until it's totally in the Light. Often clients will then see it for what it is, I just need to bring them to this point. I can then sit back and watch them unravel it.

In CBT there is a tool called ABCDE for challenging your thoughts. It brings attention to the thought process which goes like this:

> For every situation there is a thought.
>
> For every thought there is a response.
>
> Your response will give rise to an emotion.
>
> The emotion will influence your behavior.

Let's use an example:

Brenda has been seeing Robert for a few months. He has a lot of pressure at work, and told Brenda that he needs some time to gather his thoughts and work through a situation at his workplace. Truthfully, he has a disciplinary hearing, but is too ashamed to tell Brenda. However, since Brenda doesn't know the real reason, in her mind she thinks that he doesn't want to see her. She thinks the problem is *her*.

Here is how Brenda can use the ABCDE method in order to analyze her thought process:

(A) Activating Event - Describe the situation around the time her negative emotions started. What was said? Could Brenda possibly be jumping to conclusions as far as the intention behind these words? Is it possible that she may be too sensitive?

(B) Beliefs - What negative beliefs did this event trigger? Does Brenda believe something contradicting what God says about her? Could it be that this situation has very little do with her?

(C) Consequences - To which painful feelings did these beliefs or expectations lead? Brenda can rate each feeling using a scale of 1-10. (10 being extremely painful.)

(D) Dispute the Belief - Is there any evidence to show that this belief Brenda has is not true? Does she have any evidence to support what she is believing? Is she making any assumptions?

What are these assumptions? Does this belief bring her closer to healing, or does it cause more anxiety? Identify the unhelpful thought. Even if Brenda can't change the situation, how can she manage it (based on her talents, past experience, support persons, and/or resources)?

(E) Effective New Belief - What is a better way to look at this thought? It might have nothing to do with Brenda and, instead, it was actually about Robert. She can only work on her own self awareness - her thoughts, her belief, and her faith. We are all solely responsible for our own happiness, no one else is responsible for making Brenda happy. It starts with her.

Now that you've begun journaling, you will start getting to the root of your NATS (Negative Automatic Thoughts) and recognize the possible cognitive distortions through which you're viewing things. Your NATS will happen in a flash; they enter your mind very quickly, and you'll start brooding on it without realizing that you're doing it. You have planted a seed that will eventually grow. Will it be good fruit, or toxic fruit?

2 Corinthians 10 speaks of a stronghold, in other words, a fortress. When you start believing lies, it'll turn into a stronghold. The bible says we are to take our thoughts captive and put them under the obedience of Christ. When you start believing lies over what God says ... *God has forsaken me, I am separated from God, I need to do xyz to get right with God* ... All of these ideas, whether it be lies or striving, are like blocks in the wall of the stronghold. It keeps building higher and higher, and after a while you won't be able to see God for who He really is. It's important to begin taking these lies captive now, or this wall will only continue to grow in strength.

Here is where I want you to do the 3 C's:

Catch: You can catch a thought through journaling. By writing it down, you become more aware of what is going on beneath the surface. "Catching" negative thoughts and cognitive distortions means gaining an awareness of negative thinking as soon as possible. The sooner you become aware of negative thoughts that are self-denigrating, creating anxiety, or making you angry, the sooner you can begin to challenge those thoughts. Choose to become aware of the times you are engaging in negative thinking. The best time to catch yourself involved in negative inner dialogue is when you are feeling anxious, depressed, self-critical, or upset in general.

Challenge: The second step is to then challenge that thought to see if this is true. It's a lot like sitting in a courtroom, weighing up which one is wrong and which one is right. Ask yourself, "What am I telling myself that is making me feel this way?" Then ask the following questions:

1. Is this extreme thinking?

2. Is this distorted thinking? What is the evidence to confirm that your judgment is accurate? Are you using "should" statements to pressure yourself to meet self-imposed expectations that are unreasonably high?

3. Is this thinking helpful or harmful?

Change: The last thing you will do is change the thought according to what God says about it/you. Replace your negative thinking with rational statements. Begin the process of replacing all-or-nothing thinking with thoughts that may be seen from another angle. Replace personalizing thoughts with more objective statements. Here's an example:

Your child becomes very sick. You begin to question God's protection, and you start filing through your own life to see if you've somehow come up short. Unless you're perfect, you're likely to find something, likely *several* shortcomings ... so, is your child sick because of your own sins? Is God punishing you?

If you run this through your mental filters in your mind, chances are you'll start feeling very anxious. It may turn to sadness. Eventually it may turn to defensiveness and anger. *Why has this happened? What have I done?* Accusation sets in, inviting condemnation. Soon your body will begin showing signs of distress.

Just like the pony and the Thoroughbred, you'll need to decide how you will answer these cognitive distortions. Will you give up and think that the effort is just too hard? Or will you challenge your irrational thoughts and discern the lies? You discern the lies by asking yourself a couple of questions. (1) Am I assuming that I am right? and (2) Do I have the evidence to prove that there is something wrong with the pony? Am I basing the thought (he is lazy) on fact or feelings? Could I be wrong?

The more you question and challenge your thoughts and distortions, the more they will come into the Light and you will see it for what it is. The faster you take the thought captive, the easier you'll stop the snowball of negativity. Continue to place your thoughts under the obedience of Christ, and you will begin to believe what He says.

"There is therefore now no condemnation to those who are in Christ Jesus, who do not walk according to the flesh, but according to the Spirit." (Romans 8:1).

> *"For I will be merciful to their unrighteousness, and their sins and their lawless deeds I will remember no more."*
>
> (Hebrews 8:12).

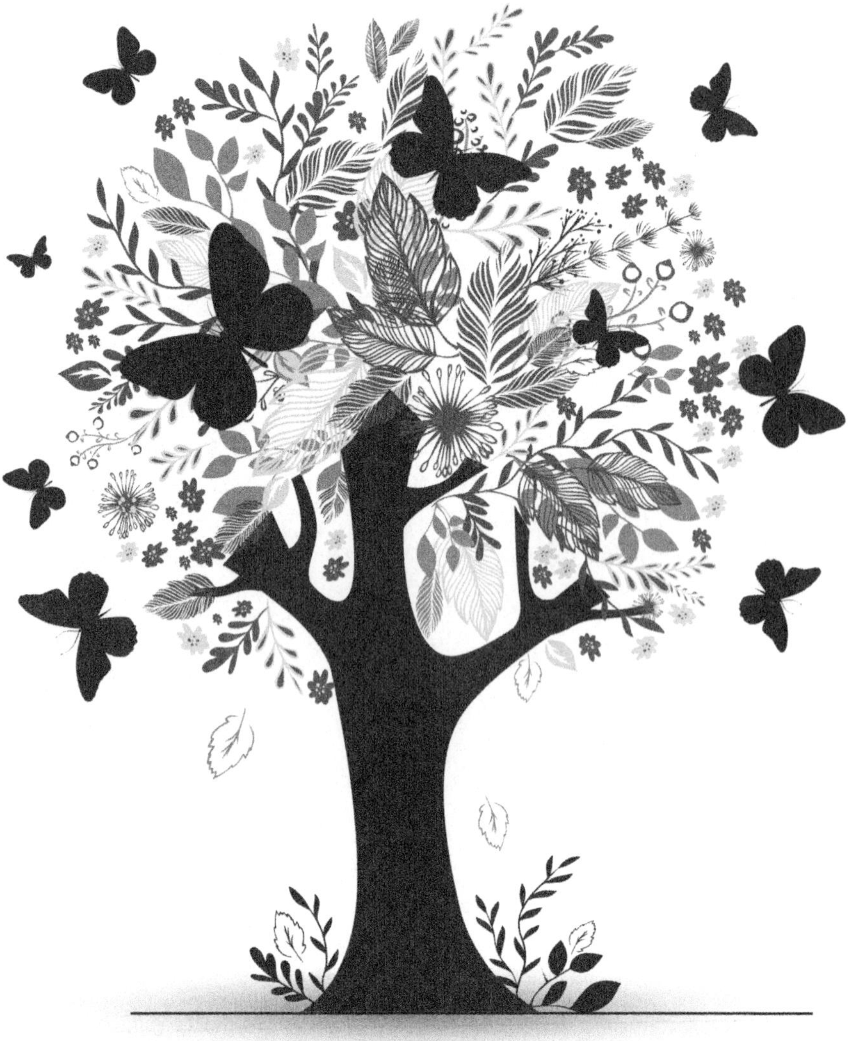

CHAPTER 8

Perception

"The outer world is a reflection of the inner world. Other people's perception of you is a reflection of them; your response to them is an awareness of you."

Roy T. Bennett, The Light in the Heart

I really do live in the back end of nowhere, and to me it's heavenly. In winter months we get a lot of rain, and what once seemed like desert turns into an oasis. I would take a back road in the morning to drive to school and to my office. Going through farms and dirt roads, me and the girls would have a lot of fun getting our pick-up really muddy. However, if the mud would stick to the windshield, it was quite the ordeal to get the clay off to be able to see where I was going. One day the same happened, and my windshield fluid was finished. I really had difficulty seeing where I was supposed to go, and it made the drive both trying and time-consuming.

I am not good with a lot of things in life, but God has given me wisdom on the body and on theology in general. Theology is like windshield wipers in your car. You need them to help you see. You use them to wipe mud off, but generally take them for granted. When the rain comes down and the mud gets stuck on the windshield, you should not be scared, because you know that you can simply switch on your wipers and they will bring clear vision. This is one of the reasons I love my work, I get to debate irrational thoughts and use theology to wipe each muddy lie away.

I can hear Him ask me, "*Do you see me, Amelia?*" Now ask yourself, are you able to see God clearly?

Have you ever given thought to your perception? Why do you believe what you believe? I think we have scarred the face of the Father without fully understanding who He really is. Let me give you an example from Genesis:

> "Then the Lord God said, 'Behold, the man has become like one of Us, to know good and evil. And now, lest he put out his hand and take also of the tree of life, and eat, and live forever"— therefore the Lord God sent him out of the garden of Eden to till the ground from which he was taken. So He drove out the man; and He placed cherubim at the east of the garden of Eden, and a flaming sword which turned every way, to guard the way to the tree of life." (Genesis 3:22-24).

Adam and Eve were like children, walking with God in a beautiful garden, no cares and no religion. After they ate from the Tree of Knowledge, they changed, and their ability to see God for who He was also changed. **Adam and Eve hid from God, not because God changed toward them after their sin, but because their view of God had changed.** Their view of Him changed from a loving Father to a God they had to try to please. In their minds, God was measuring them by their own righteousness and now it was their burden to work on it. The change in their relationship was *in their mind* alone. After all, they hid from God; He did not hide from them.

So why did God banish them from the garden? It wasn't because He was mean; it was to guard the way to the tree of life. Here is the greatest lesson in our God's nature: the way to Him isn't by attaining some form of godliness on your own; it's by seeing Him for who He is—Love. He was guarding the very definition of relationship in the most existential form, guarding it from anything that fell short of who He is. Unashamed Love is what leads us back to the tree of life, and He didn't want it any other way. Christ is that way. "God is love" (1 John 4:16) and "this is love, not that we loved God, but that He loved us and sent His Son to be the propitiation for our sins" (1 John 4:10).

He banished them from the garden because they would never see Him for who He was. They had become blind, and He would restore their sight in time. They were never separated from Him, they were alienated in their minds. "And you, who once were alienated and enemies *in your mind* by wicked works, yet now He has reconciled in the body of His flesh through death, to present you holy, and blameless, and above reproach in His sight" (Colossians 1:21-22).

When they left the garden, He followed them. He never turned His back on them, but walked with them. He fed them in the desert. He gave them shelter. He protected them. Eventually, the Son of God would open their eyes, the veil would be lifted, and we would be welcomed into the glorious Kingdom.

We were probably taught that God needed to punish Adam and Eve because they did not listen and from there on we formed a lot of our theology. Weighing up everything we know now, is there a possibility that we may have been wrong? Maybe this is something you've never thought about, so I challenge you now to think about what He has done for you.

How you interpret events in the Bible will determine your take on who God is. A good place to start your walk is the book of John in the New Testament. The book of John differs from the gospels of Luke, Mark and Matthew which were written in a very Jewish way and spoke of the genealogy of Jesus and His right to be King. Matthew 1, for instance, begins, "This is the genealogy of Jesus the Messiah, the son of David, the son of Abraham..." (Matthew 1:1). It speaks about His birth, His ministry and death.

John, on the other hand, had a very special relationship with Jesus. He saw something that the other disciples did not see.

"In the beginning was the Word, and the Word was with God, and the Word was God. He was in the beginning with God. All things were made through Him, and without Him nothing was made that was made. In Him was life, and the life was the light of men. And the light shines in the darkness, and the darkness did not comprehend it" (John 1:1-5).

JOHN'S WITNESS: THE TRUE LIGHT

"There was a man sent from God, whose name was John. This man came for a witness, to bear witness of the Light, that all through him might believe. He was not that Light, but was sent to bear witness of that Light. That was the true Light which gives light to every man coming into the world. He was in the world, and the world was made through Him, and the world did not know Him. He came to His own, and His own did not receive Him. But as many as received Him, to them He gave the right to become children of God, to those who believe in His name: who were born, not of blood, nor of the will of the flesh, nor of the will of man, but of God." (John 1:6-13).

1 John 1:1-2 similarly reveals an intimacy, a relationship that is deeply personal to him. "We proclaim to you the One who existed from the beginning, whom *we have heard and seen*. We saw *Him with our own eyes* and *touched Him with our own hands*. And this is the life that was revealed; *we have seen it* and testified to it, and we proclaim to you the eternal life that was with the Father and was revealed to us..." (emphasis added).

John speaks of the beginning, that beautiful unity—the fellowship in the beginning and them being face to face. The Word was with the Father and that "with" is so beautiful, the only way you can explain it is by saying they are One.

In the beginning was the Word and the Word was with God and God was the Word. Then he repeats it ... He was with God in the beginning. Perfect Oneness. There is no distance between them. Through Him all things were made, not one thing came into being not by his hands ...more repetition, almost like he knew we would not get it. What is John saying here?

Jesus is the Creator.

John is shouting to the world that the Creator has stepped into Creation and made *us* a part of their relationship. That is what you get to share in, the beautiful relationship of the Trinity. You are adopted into the family of the Father, Son and Spirit, and because they live forever and they abide in you, you get to live with them and share whatever they have. Isn't it wonderful to know that we also have a seat at the table? John gives us a totally different view of God, a different frame in which we can see we are one with Him. He lovingly reconciled us to Him.

CORE BELIEFS

There are 3 different levels of cognition: (1) Core beliefs, (2) Dysfunctional assumptions, and (3) Negative Automatic Thoughts

Core beliefs are a person's most central ideas about themselves, others, and the world. These beliefs act like a lens through which every situation and life experience is seen. Because of this, people with different core beliefs might be in the same situation, yet think, feel, and behave very differently.

To simplify this, core beliefs are like sunglasses. If they are rose tinted, everything you see will be rose tinted. What if they are scratched? Chances are that you might notice them in the very beginning, but your eyes will adjust to the scratches and after some time you won't even see them. Your brain is like the lens, and the scratch is the core belief. Harmful core beliefs lead to negative thoughts, feelings, and behaviors, whereas rational core beliefs lead to balanced reactions. They shape our reality and modify our thinking and our behavior. In fact, nothing matters more than our core beliefs.

Many times we perceive things as little children and try to rationalize it. A child may see Mommy and Daddy never having time to play with him, but his rational brain has not developed yet. He doesn't understand the immense pressure they are under in trying to juggle work and personal life. All he sees is that they don't have time for him. He might even believe it's his fault. Years later he will still struggle with this. His core belief has been shaped as a child, and he dare not question it.

His core belief says *I am not worthy enough for others to spend time with me*. For every situation, every time life disappoints him, he will interpret life through the belief that 'I am not worthy for others to spend time with me'. Core beliefs are many times the causes of our problems, including our negative automatic thoughts. It's seen as absolute truth and that belief itself isn't questioned, yet it is the springboard for all your subsequent thoughts. In other words, it is at the root of your thoughts. All our thoughts filter through our core beliefs. The external information we take in will 'consult' with our core belief and from there it will form our perceived reality.

A core belief is just what the name implies—it's a *belief* rather than a fact. Based on childhood assessments, they are often untrue. They are constant and relentless. We "fuel" them with evidence to reinforce the core belief, and they repel anything that might challenge them. Just because you believe it does not make it true. The good news is that it is possible to change them.

Here are a few examples of Core beliefs:

- I am worthless.
- If someone will really get to know me, they'll lose interest.
- The world is dangerous; I always need to be on guard.
- People are out to get me.

Core beliefs not only determine how we see the world, they also shape how we believe the world sees us. Where do you see yourself in the world? Do you feel safe? Do you feel loved? Do you BELONG?

If I can help you change your core beliefs in order that you may know that you BELONG, most of the battle is won. Now that you know you belong, automatically you know your worth as a person, and it cultivates a better sense of self-esteem. You need to change your core belief to 'I am loved. I am enough. I belong.'

Let's look at ways to manage the core beliefs about yourself:

IDENTIFY THE BELIEF AS A NON-FACT

Anytime you bring up a core belief, ask yourself to explore the evidence against it. If you were to use the belief "I am rejected", identify your accomplishments and challenges you've overcome, no matter how small you think they may be. Ask yourself, "Which of my experiences proves that this belief is not completely true all the time?" Identifying these will weaken your belief. Recognize that this belief is a feeling rather than a fact. Just changing the wording from "I am rejected" to "I feel like I am rejected" allows the mind to see this belief as more subjective.

EXPLORE YOUR LIFE WITHOUT THE NEGATIVE BELIEF

Explore how your life would be different if you did not have the negative belief. How would your life change if you realize how loved you are, when you realize how important you are to Him. If we were able to take care of our negative thoughts and replace them with healthy positive thoughts, we would truly feel what it means to be free.

TRY TO DEFINE THE BELIEF

You might believe that everyone is rejecting you. Can you define that? Let's use an example: Your daughter comes home from school and does not want to talk to you. Maybe she slams the door shut and turns up the music. Your immediate reaction is to get angry, maybe you feel disrespected. Maybe it reminds you of something that happened in your childhood and it resembles the same feelings you had at that time. You may at that moment feel that it's rejection, but are you looking at the full picture? She might have had a fight with her best friend and she's not up to talking to anyone. She might need some time alone just to quiet her thoughts. It has nothing to do with rejection, but because this scenario runs through your mental filters and you are sensitive to this, you will automatically assume the worst. Step out of the situation and look at it from another angle. What is it that you don't see?

CORE BELIEF WORKSHEET

Take some time to self-reflect and consider the following questions.

1. Where would you like to have closure?

2. What is stopping you from having that closure?

3. What are you holding onto that you can choose to release?

4. Are you holding back forgiveness towards anyone? If so, why?

5. How much time are you using to think about the past or worrying about the future?

6. If you think about a certain event in the past, would you say it's hindering you from moving forward in life?

7. Are you waiting for someone else to take responsibility for the situation?

8. What areas of your life do you need to give more attention?

9. Would you say fear is holding you back in any way?

10. In what areas are you spending too much time on things that are not your priorities?

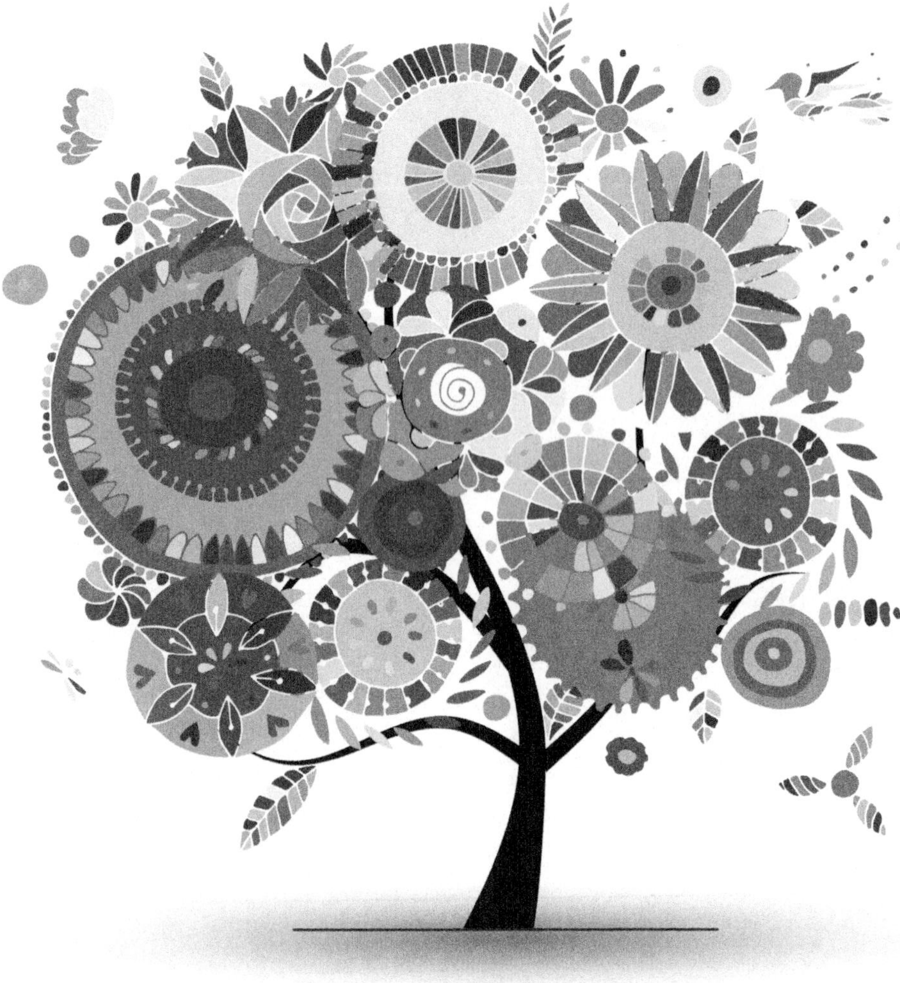

CHAPTER 9

The Waymaker

> *"I will go before you and make the crooked places straight; I will break in pieces the gates of bronze and cut the bars of iron."*
> (Isaiah 45:2)

If you know some church history, you'll recognize that I lean to the Eastern Orthodox view. Even if you don't, I want to encourage you to continue reading. I am not trying to deceive you, or even get you to understand my point of view. I am here to present my views and experiences, and then it is for you to make up your mind about everything else.

Putting my girls to bed, they would love to hear about John the Baptist, and many nights I would read the story to them:

> "Then Jesus came from Galilee to the Jordan to be baptized by John. But John tried to deter him, saying, 'I need to be baptized by you, and do you come to me?' Jesus replied, 'Let it be so now; it is proper for us to do this to fulfill all righteousness.' Then John consented. As soon as Jesus was baptized, he went up out of the water. At that moment heaven was opened, and he saw the Spirit of God descending like a dove and alighting on him. And a voice from heaven said, 'This is my Son, whom I love; with him I am well pleased.'" (Matthew 3:13-17).

The baptism of John was for repentance, so why exactly did Jesus get baptized? He had no sin; he didn't need to be baptized. When we look at the bigger picture and the incarnation of Christ, we understand that we are one with Christ—in fact, we no longer live, but it's Him who lives in us. Why did He get baptized? He did it for us! Don't get me wrong, I believe we all should get baptized, I am just trying to expand your thinking.

Question: When did you get baptized?

Answer: 2,000 and some years ago ... the moment when Jesus walked into the Jordan river. He left no stone unturned, He left no loose ends, and He left nothing to chance. He took our filthy robes and made us beautiful.

What then happens to those who never get the chance to get baptized today? The baby who dies in the womb? The mind who is tormented by suicidal ideation and in which no light ever breaks the prison of their own mind? What about the adult in a mental ward who can't even fathom who God is? What happens to them?

They have been forgiven and washed. He took the sins of the world upon Himself, swallowed death in victory, and He reigns victorious. Everything is in Him, nothing is outside of Him. John the Baptist prepared the way for us to receive Jesus, and Jesus prepared the way for us to receive His kingdom, all He is, and restore all that we had lost, even more.

When you understand that you are one with Christ, you understand that you walked into the river with Him. Everything Jesus did was intentional. He went before us to make the crooked places straight and to break down any bars that hold us captive. When you choose to walk with Him, He has already prepared the way. He *is* the Way.

Ephesians 4:4-6 states, "There is one body and one Spirit, just as you were called in one hope of your calling; one Lord, one faith, one baptism; one God and Father of all, who is above all, and through all, and in you all."

GOD ENTERED OUR FLESH

It feels like we walk into a new reality in the New Testament, a truth and a mystery far beyond our understanding. After everything we learn in the Old Testament, we then come upon this shocking revelation by Jesus that "No one knows the Father except the Son" (Matthew 11:27). No one. This statement certainly did not sit well with the Pharisees. Jesus dared stand up and proclaim this truth—they all had it wrong! In fact, the teachers had no idea what they were talking about!

How could it be that the most learned teachers of the law still didn't know the Father? Have you ever thought about this? The relationship inside the Trinity is so beautiful that none of us will get it.

Perhaps this example will help: What if I was told that I could have a relationship with a cloud? Yes, a cloud! Personally, I don't know much about clouds, so I would probably start by studying nephology. After that, I could at least start to talk about some aspects of a cloud. I might even appear to be really intelligent on the subject. However, I would still only be able to explain things I've heard about the cloud either from outside observance or from a textbook that someone else has written. In other words, I could start listing details from my perspective, but none of it is intimate knowledge or understanding, and certainly not enough to feel the sense of relationship. I could attempt to sit amongst the clouds to create some sort of bond ... hmm ... even that proves difficult. It's kind of hard to form an intimate bond with a cloud. Why? Even when I try to be in the midst of the clouds, it doesn't seem to have any real "substance" with which I can identify. The real problem is that we are not of the same substance. I am human and a cloud.... well...it's a cloud.

It's the same in the Trinity. We can have our studies in theology, and our ideas on atonement, but Jesus tells us that He is the only one who knows who the Father is. We cannot get to know the love of the Father without knowing who Jesus is, because it's a closed loop, it does not change. God had to cross this bridge and become human, otherwise we would not get it.

God is Spirit and we are in our human bodies. How will we get to know who and how God is? You can't imagine the Father, you can only imagine Jesus. It's inconceivable for you to know God, because He is Uncreated and you are created. I ask again, how will we get to know who God is?

God becomes one of us and tells us *when you see me, you see the Father* (John 14:9). He also says that He doesn't do anything He does not see the Father do (John 5:19). In other words, when Jesus was healing, He was seeing the Father healing. When Jesus had grace towards a certain woman, the Father had grace towards her. He cried with the sisters of Lazarus, as He saw the Father also cry with compassion.

PARTICIPATION IN THE WAY, THE TRUTH, AND THE LIFE_

There is an analogy I always use in describing what Christ has done for us. I grab a cup of coffee and begin like this: Let's say that I made this cup of coffee. I love this coffee! The problem is that when I taste it, I realize the milk has gone sour. How can I "unsour" this coffee? I, Amelia, become the coffee. I jump into the mug and become the coffee. Then I change the milk, make sure it's good, and jump out again. I am still holding the cup of coffee in my hand. That is how mind-boggling the Incarnation of Christ is! When you understand the depth of what He has done, it will change you forever.

Christ brings us the knowledge of the Father. When we participate in the Light of Christ, we partake in the Father, because Jesus is the eternal Word coming from the *being* of the Father. How do we participate? We mirror Him through loving the lost, healing the sick, and drawing closer to God. When we participate in love, the Spirit opens our eyes ... and shows us that Christ is inside of us, and that Christ is the anointed one and we are just the vehicle. As we step into (or surrender to) the love of Christ, the Spirit anoints us to participate with Christ in that love. The participation is within relationality.

At times I would walk around and not even notice that people with crutches were being healed without me doing anything. This happens because I am always in prayer, I am always thinking, and I am always praising. We are not anointed, we are human. Jesus is the anointed One, and we participate in His Life and Love.

Want to know more of Jesus? Want to have more knowledge and more wisdom? Invite the Holy Spirit, because He is the One who glorifies Christ. That's what the Spirit does, He opens your eyes to show you who Jesus is. John 15:26 states, "when the Helper comes, whom I shall send to you from the Father, the Spirit of truth who proceeds from the Father, *He* will testify of Me." John 14:26 similarly states that it is "the Helper, the Holy Spirit, whom the Father will send in My name, He will teach you all things, and bring to your remembrance all things that I said to you."

The Amplified Bible describes the expanse of who God is beautifully, "No one has seen God [His essence, His divine nature] at any time; the [One and] only begotten God [that is, the unique Son] who is in the intimate presence of the Father, He has explained Him [and interpreted and revealed the awesome wonder of the Father]" (1 John 4:12). We aren't able to comprehend all of who He is on our own. It is Jesus who makes us a part of their relationship (John 17:20).

The Creator took on our flesh and made the way. Christ takes what He has and gives it to us through the Spirit. As He is always with the Father, in fact He is sitting in the *bosom* of the Father (John 1:18), He then shares what He has with us. He shares the love and the communion with us through the Spirit.

In my own life, I've experienced how witnessing genuine love is in itself the best invitation into a relationship. Both of my daughters are very social creatures, they would love nothing more than to have the whole world over at our house. They would organize pool parties, inviting anyone who wants to come. Children of all backgrounds would come to visit, and at my house there's no thought to who's in the "popular" crowd and who's not.

The kids would turn the music up loud, start dancing, and jump into the pool. I loved treating them with sweets, cool drinks, and crisps. I'd sit by the pool and watch them enjoy life, and that in turn gave me great joy.

At some point, my daughters would come sit on my lap and hug me, and I would cuddle with them. Because of what my kids did, their friends would also come and sit close to me, then closer, and later they were on my lap, too. After a while they would giggle like my kids and hug me.

It was because of my kids that they felt welcome to hug me, participating in the love that He generates within me. If it wasn't for my Luna, they would never just come and sit on my lap. I have no relationship with them, but I have a very close bond to my daughters. The relationship with my daughters is ours, it does not change. Through my daughters, these children were able to participate in the love we have, they were able to join the party. That is what the Son of God did. He revealed the intimate nature of the Father, made others feel welcome, and invited them to participate. He made you a part of that life, and it is eternal.

GRACE MEETS US WHERE WE ARE

Maybe you've been that person who desperately wants to participate, to feel welcome in a relationship, to feel the hug of someone who genuinely cares about you. Maybe witnessing genuine love isn't enough of an invitation, because you simply feel like you don't deserve it. Maybe there's just too much wrong with you—is that what you're thinking? I have news for you. Grace wouldn't be grace if you deserved it. Grace meets you exactly where you are. When all the accusations are chasing you down, I know the One who will stand between you and the accuser ... even if the accuser is yourself.

Let me share one of my favorite passages of Scripture (I have many favorites). Jesus was teaching in the temple when a group of scribes and Pharisees brought a woman before him.

Throughout Jesus' ministry, many were brought before him. Each of those people had been in need. They needed healing, they needed deliverance, they needed to be set free. In short, they needed life. This time was different, or so these religious leaders thought. This time they wanted to see him bring death.

The woman had been caught in the very act of adultery, and Mosaic Law called for death. Would Jesus sentence her to stoning? Either way He answered, they figured they'd caught Him in a trap. Did they have their rocks already in hand?

Christ is called our Rock and our Salvation. Think about that when picturing the day when, instead of picking up a rock to condemn the woman caught in adultery, He somehow convinced everyone to drop theirs. How did it happen? He had bent down to write in the sand.

"Let him who is without sin among you be the first to throw a stone at her," Jesus replied, and again, Jesus started writing on the ground. One by one they began walking away, until her accusers were gone and only Jesus remained.

"Has no one condemned you?"

"No one, Lord." she replied.

"Neither do I condemn you; go, and from now on sin no more."

This story from John 8 ends at verse 11. But wait, there is more..

When Jesus spoke again to the people, He said, "I am the light of the world. Whoever follows me will not walk in darkness, but will have the light of life" (John 8:12).

When you start following Him, you won't fall around in darkness. You'll know exactly where to go to get to the kitchen, you'll have the Light of life, a Lamp at your feet guiding you.

Ever wondered what Jesus wrote in the ground? Speculation really, no one knows. What matters is that everyone who comes before Him is in need, and He chooses Life.

> "Lord, you are the hope of Israel; all who forsake you will be put to shame. Those who turn away from you will be written in the dust, because they have forsaken the Lord, the spring of living water."
>
> - Jeremiah 17:13

THE HIDDEN KINGDOM

What if the kingdom is inside of everyone, no matter who they are, but few find it? You need to be like a child to get in. You need to shrink, be small, worry less, and be less consumed with the problems of today.

My children wake up in the morning knowing they will be given breakfast; they can even decide what they want. I know their specific preferences, and I'll cater to their needs and wants. They don't care about money or politics. They are not worried about tomorrow. Their biggest hurdle for the day is probably what game they will play next. They don't understand the logistics of time management or juggling work.

They know that when school closes for the day, I'm at the gate waiting for them. When they jump, I'll catch them. When they're hungry, I will feed them. And when they fall, I will pick them up.

The kingdom of God is beautiful, and that very kingdom is inside of you, but few find it. It's a place where streams of living water flow; it's a kingdom where the sick are healed and where the impossible happens, but you need to be like a child to get in. You need to shrink, become smaller, be humble...

How do you enter? There is a door to this kingdom that you're not strong enough to open; you were never intended to be. Instead, you enter through Jesus, "the door of the sheep" (John 10:7). He is the Way (John 14:6) and through the blood of Jesus, we enter the Holy place. (Hebrews 10:9). It is a powerful kingdom hidden inside of you, and your entry is granted by the Creator. He is the door to the Kingdom, and the Way, and the Life.

Question:

1. What area/situation in your life do you feel judged?

2. Why do you condemn yourself when He doesn't?

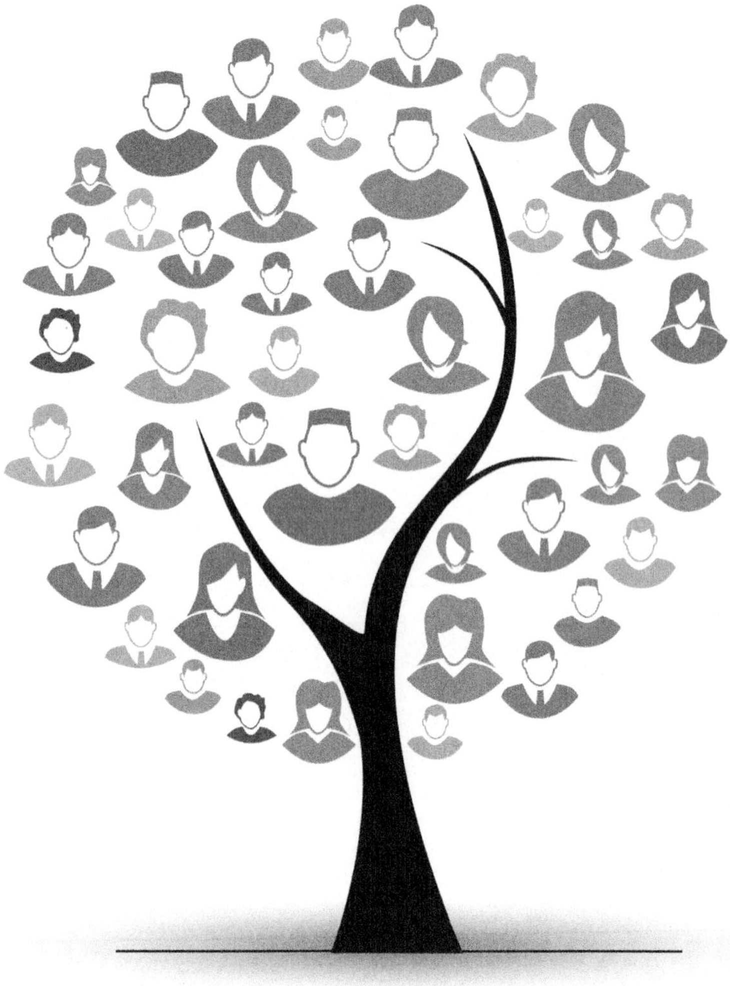

CHAPTER 10

The Family Tree:

OUR PURPOSE AND CALLING

"I am the vine, you are the branches."

(John 15:5)

Humanity as a whole craves meaning; we crave to know our purpose. What is *your* purpose?

Christians look at the Bible to find answers. I believe much of the Western Church has the gospel the wrong way around. It's not about you letting Jesus into your heart, it's about Jesus who made a place for you inside of Him and invites you to share in the relationship of the Trinity.

Let's go to where it speaks of the beginning of creation.

Looking at Genesis, it will tell you the story of Adam and Eve, and about a garden God made for them. It also gives a picture of Old Testament life, but it does not give you the answer to what our meaning or purpose is.

If we continue our search through the Bible for further references to the "beginning", we may take note of John the Apostle's opening notes, "In the beginning was the Word, and the Word was with God, and the Word was God." (John 1:1). John speaks about a beautiful relationship between the Father and the Son. It really is so close, the only way you can describe it is ONE. They are inside of each other, never getting lost and always being the Father, the Son, and the Spirit.

While the Word (Logos) was holding everything together, He stepped into time and space and became flesh. This is the gospel. The Uncreated became part of the created, so that the created could become part of the Uncreated. You have been transformed into a new being. Does this change into a "new creation" describe our purpose?

There are verses which speak of something that happened even before creation, a purpose and a calling that is so much bigger than we ever thought, a purpose and a calling that is outside of time and space. It speaks of a Love that made a decision, not based on who we were, but on who He is. It is as though God had a meeting before creation and decided upon a plan. God would never leave us to self-destruct, and that is why Jesus jumped into time and space and became one of us.

2 Timothy 1:9 -

> "... who has saved us and called us with a holy calling, not according to our works, but according to His own purpose and grace *which was given to us in Christ Jesus before time began.*"

Read it again a few times.

He gave us everlasting life and drew us to Himself by HIS calling. His calling is Holy. His calling is not from this cosmos, nor from this creation; His calling is not contained within these—it's something much bigger. In fact it is so big that it's outside of time and space!

His calling wasn't based upon anything we have done. Grace is a gift; it is not awarded to us by anything good we've done, nor is it withheld from us because of any of the wrong we've done. Romans 3:23 says that we "all have sinned and fall short of the glory of God." So, thank goodness for the Son of God!

Grace confirms our union with Jesus—EVEN BEFORE TIME BEGAN! Grace is not by anything you've done, but by a decision

THEY have made. You can't earn grace. You don't choose it, either. You wake up in it!

Oh, dear ... we've had it wrong all along? In our minds we think that we will "make Jesus king of our lives", but He is already king. We think that we "ask Jesus into our hearts", when He already holds our very being and heart together. We think that we "make Him a part of our life", when He is the one who's called us to participate in His Life which is eternal in union with the Father and the Spirit. We get to be a part of the beautiful unity of the Trinity? Yes, we do!

Could this be our purpose and our calling? To know we belong to Him and to introduce others to this beautiful Light that is the true essence of the Father? Remember, the Light is on in the kitchen, and He is calling you out of darkness to come and sit with Him. It's not a matter of being inside the house or outside; it's about *are you participating in the relationship?* If you're able to see the Light in the kitchen, you can run to Him. You are no longer in a kingdom of darkness and deception, but you are in the Kingdom of Light where you have sight and you can participate.

Paul's message to King Agrippa regarding his conversion further demonstrates how God's Light has always existed within darkness. The darkness is really just having our eyes shut. However, that's not how most modern theologians describe Him. Let's check out Acts 26:17-18. This was the message Jesus gave to Paul regarding the Gentiles: "... I now send you, to open their eyes, *in order* to turn *them* from darkness to light, and *from* the power of Satan to God, that they may receive forgiveness of sins and an inheritance among those who are sanctified by faith in Me." It's worth highlighting that this was Paul recounting the words of Jesus.

In this passage, did Paul say, "I was called to un-separate people from God and to teach them how to get Jesus inside of them"? NO.

In the garden humanity became blind, and God knew this. In our lives today, He knew we'd fall short. If you are a parent and your child is starting to walk, do you get upset each time your child falls? Do you kick her while she is down? No, she is learning, and you know that in the end she will get it right. So when she falls, you help her up. Where there are bumps and bruises, you kiss them.

While we were in darkness, while we were too blind to see who God was, He stepped into the darkness as a Light that no man could dim and He keeps shining in the darkness. Even while we did not get it, He chose to take the bill.

Ephesians says we were chosen to be adopted before the beginning of creation; even before Genesis, we were to be in the family of God. When you are adopted, you share in the life of that adoptive family. Thus, we are to share in the Life of God. But wait! Doesn't this sound like the same temptation the snake presented in Eden? Wasn't this desire to participate in "Godliness" the hubris that set everything off on the wrong course? The devil really is in the details...

What if God never wanted us to know the details of right versus wrong? What if He never wanted us to bear the weight of good versus bad judgments? What if we were made to simply walk by the Spirit and not live by picking apart every detail of ethics and morality? Sound crazy? These judgments are all due to the knowledge of good and evil ... that same tree God warned us to stay clear of.

Now we have become like God, since we possess the knowledge of good and evil. That sounds like a big statement, I know. Look at what God said after they ate from the tree: "Then the Lord God said, "Behold, the man has become like one of Us, to know good and evil." (Genesis 3:22). However, this particular result isn't cause for celebration.

Although we were already made in His image, God wanted to protect humanity from this particular "lens" through which we would then see the world. While God may still see perfectly with this understanding, our vision, on the other hand, becomes tainted. It's like putting on someone else's prescription glasses—it hurts your eyes. If you have small children, you can relate. Ever see something show up on the television that was not meant for children, or something age restricted, etc.? What do you do? You turn off the TV and tell your child that they don't need to worry about it. Really, you don't want them to have to deal with something like that while they are so young. You protect them.

From then on, a veil covered the eyes of Adam and Eve and they could not see God for who He was. Their vision darkened. From that point on, **humanity has used a tree which God forbade us to eat from—used it to judge Him, and eventually used that same tree to kill Him, the Author of Life.**

While we were too blind to see who God was, He stepped into the darkness as a Light that no man could dim. Darkness doesn't scare Him; His love sees through it all. Romans 5:8 reveals that "But God demonstrates his own love for us in this: While we were still sinners, Christ died for us." He doesn't love us once our eyes are opened. He doesn't love us once we're all cleaned up. *While we were still sinners* ... that is the nature of Jesus; that's how beautiful He really is.

I once heard a testimony of a woman who had been orphaned. In heartbreaking detail she described the feelings she would go through each time a new couple entered the orphanage. The door would open to reveal men and women wearing warm smiles and nice, clean clothing. Their eyes would span over the children, and every time their eyes met hers, her heart would cry, *pick me, pick me*. Yet, it didn't matter how well behaved she tried to be, time after time, that heart was broken. A voice in her head began screaming: *Nobody wants you! You're ugly! You're dirty! You're stupid! No one is ever going to pick you - never*. A broken heart will try to protect itself, try to replace pain with anger, try to act like it doesn't care. But try as she might, it continued the cry, *choose me*.

I wish I could end the story with the happy couple finally locking eyes on her and swooping her into their loving family. It didn't happen that way. All she knew was rejection. She was a dirty, ugly, angry child with a foul mouth, as she described, but in that mess she found the One whose eyes didn't pass her by. In her worst state possible, she finally felt ... chosen. Her anger didn't scare Him. Her dirtiness didn't disgust Him. Her foul mouth didn't offend Him. She saw His love and grace for what it was, wholly unconditional. His light shone through her darkness. She is not the exception. It is through His goodwill and grace that each one of us is adopted.

How many of you have felt that God averts His eyes from you? Or that He looks at you with displeasure? After all, He is too holy to look upon sin. Ever heard that? I'm guessing many of you have, since this is a common teaching. Habakkuk 1:13 states, "Your eyes are too pure to look on evil; you cannot tolerate wrongdoing." Many people use this verse to say that God is too holy to look at you, a sinner, but when you read this chapter in context, it actually says the opposite. It's a cry to God saying that God is too holy to just sit back and not do anything about it.

Here's an example: I am a good mother, therefore, I won't just watch my children being bullied by someone. I'll step in! That is the meaning of the verse. The Lamb was slain before creation began; there was a plan for your existence and for your salvation before anything else. If the Lamb was slain before creation began, it means that you were forgiven long before you were born. You were forgiven even before your repentance.

I have a signature perfume. It's one of the few things I spend money on, and it's one of the most expensive perfumes I have. I was given a bottle as a present, and it always stood on my bedside table. It was a screw-top bottle and was really pretty. This was one of the best gifts I ever received.

One day, I walked out of the room to make a cup of coffee. Upon my return, I found my 2-year-old daughter emptying the last bit of perfume onto her head. I was too late! What could I do? She didn't fully understand what she had done; she was only two. No matter how valuable that bottle of perfume was to me, there is nothing she could do to make me love her any less ... nothing in this world can stop my love for her.

When I had my children in my tummy, they were pre-forgiven. They were forgiven before they even knew about anything. So after I watched the last precious drops of perfume emptied out, I took a deep breath and later bought another bottle with my own money. I took the bill. That is what love does. It covers everything.

While you were a toddler, walking around and throwing expensive perfume over your head, God knew you wouldn't comprehend it, and He took the bill. Welcome to the family!

Question:

1. Do you have a clear vision of your purpose?

2. How often do you judge yourself or others with a limited perspective?

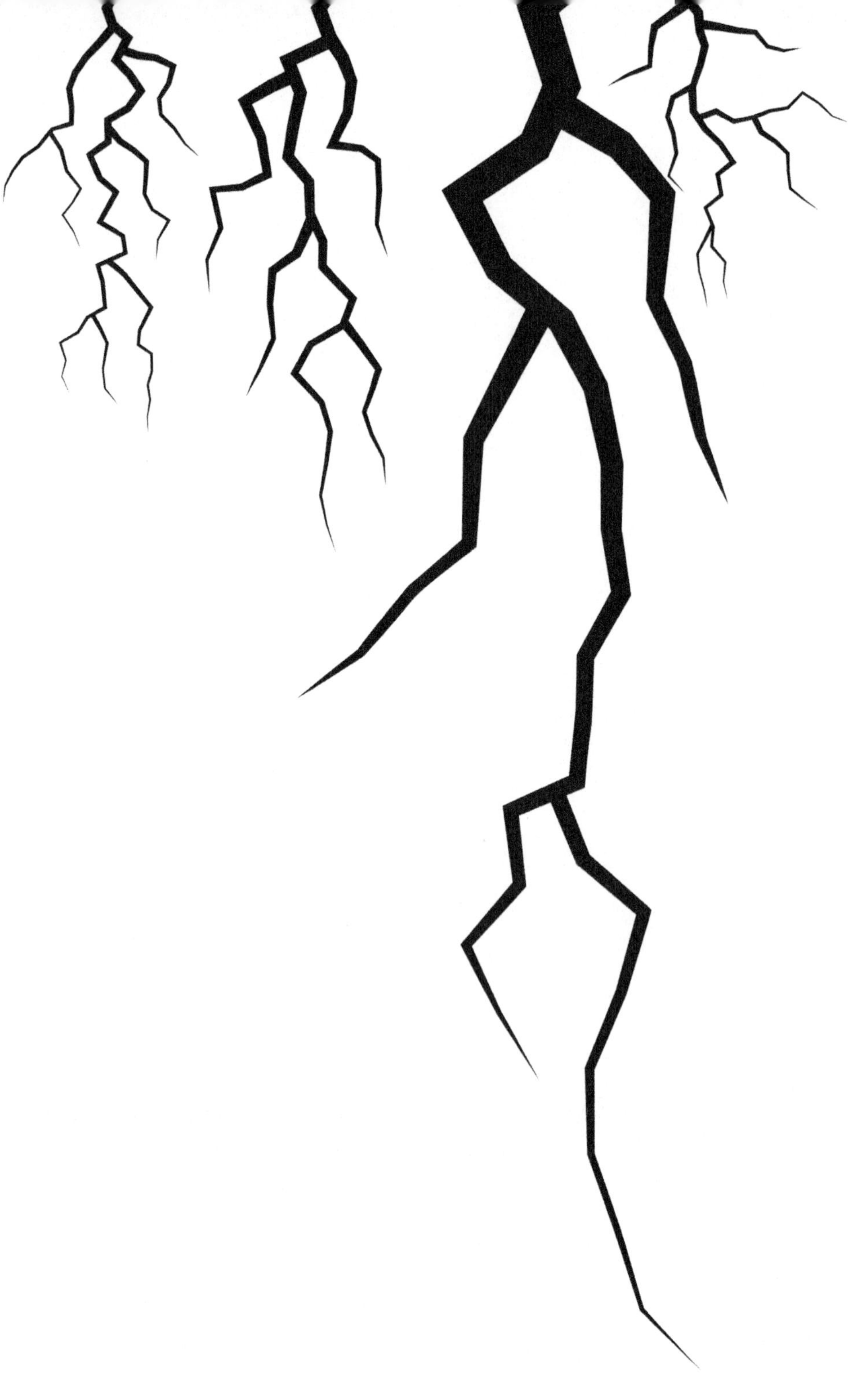

CHAPTER 11

The Darkness of Dualism

"And if a house is divided against itself, that house cannot stand."

(Mark 3:25)

Clients come to see me and I hear their desperation, "Please help me! How did I get to this point in my life?" I'll listen to what they tell me and, after some time, I ask them: "Why do you believe it? Is there evidence to prove you are unattractive, not good enough, rejected, etc.?" They will reply that they have none.

Why do you believe what you believe?

God opened my eyes and showed me that when I look at something within the wrong frame, I'll end up with the wrong end of the stick. For example, let's say you are baking a chocolate cake. Sounds easy enough, right? What if you accidentally put two cups of salt into the cake instead of two cups of sugar? Same ingredients, only wrong portions. Can it really make much of a difference? Absolutely! That is what happens when you have the wrong framework concerning the work of Christ. Christians are so obsessed with separation, but if we start with a frame of separation, we end up with inedible cake.

The work of Christ is universal, meaning that what He has done has such a massive impact on creation that it affects every single person on this earth. We start off being inside of God, reconciled to the heart of the Father. We don't start off separated and then, by a series of steps, we get saved—that is Greek philosophy, whose roots run very deep in dualism.

Let me explain what dualism means. *Dualism* simply means dividing things, particularly opposing things, so in the example of religion it would frame everything up with this belief that there are two gods, divided, fighting each other for a prize. You might think this seems reasonable; after all, Satan is fighting against God! But Satan cannot exist outside of God. Every battle Satan wages is still within the realms which God created. Satan can't run and escape to his own realm, out of the reach of God. It simply can't be divided in this way. Satan isn't that powerful.

A dualistic mindset splits things up, and it doesn't end with the division between God and Satan, it also creates division amongst ourselves. I can believe that you are separated from God, and believe that I am not. This would mean that I am "in" and you are "out". Now I can treat you as though you are my enemy. I can treat you like a criminal. I can hate you, objectify you, or vilify you. This mindset begins with separation and has to cross over to union.

However, when we start with union, it gives us another frame. We start off reconciled at the cross. "God was in Christ reconciling the world to Himself, not imputing their trespasses to them, and has committed to us the word of reconciliation" (2 Corinthians 5:19). Read it. Read it. Read it. Then read it again. There is no division of people according to those who are separated from God and those who are reconciled. We are *all* reconciled, the whole world. We are all forgiven. Whether we accept forgiveness and want a relationship is up to us.

In the philosophy of the mind, dualism would mean that the body and the mind are separate. In Christianity, dualism somehow even manages to divide the Trinity. If we believe that God can't look at sin, and Jesus became sin ... what then? 2 Corinthians 5:21 tells us that "He made Him who knew no sin to *be* sin for us, that we might become the righteousness of God in Him." In keeping within the dualistic frame, we suddenly have a Father who made Jesus become sin, but is then so disgusted by him that He forsakes that Son on the cross.

The Father never left Jesus while he was at the cross. The Father was inside the Son, busy reconciling the world to Him. He took on our sin. He took on our diseases. He took on our shame. He took on the very darkness that began when Adam and Eve hid, breaking through the net in which the father of lies had caught humankind, "My God, My God, why have you forsaken me?" (Psalm 22:1 and Matthew 27:46). He has not forsaken us. Never will He leave us, nor forsake us. And He leaves us this beautiful message—You don't have to climb your way to Me; I've made you holy through my Son. *You are reconciled.* That's your message. Go tell the world!

You have been reconciled. Whoever you are and whatever your denomination is, there is no "in" or "out". You will be in His presence, whether you like it or not. There is no place you can go that He is not:

> "Where can I go from Your Spirit? Or where can I flee from Your presence? If I ascend into heaven, You are there; if I make my bed in hell, behold, You are there. If I take the wings of the morning, and dwell in the uttermost parts of the sea, even there Your hand shall lead me, and Your right hand shall hold me. If I say, "Surely the darkness shall fall on me," Even the night shall be light about me; indeed, the darkness shall not hide from You, but the night shines as the day; the darkness and the light are both alike to You." (Psalm 139:7-12).

Dualism continues the idea of separation into the afterlife. If you're separated from God before death, then surely this separation continues after death. Is this dualistic framework consistent with Scripture? The aforementioned Psalm certainly seems to refute it. Revelation 14:10 also seems to fly in the face of dualism. Here's what happens to those who worship the beast: "He shall be tormented with fire and brimstone *in the presence of the holy angels and in the presence of the Lamb.*" Whatever your concept is of heaven or hell, it will be in the Presence of Him.

Contrary to popular belief, hell isn't the devil's playground; it's not his turf. Also contrary to popular teaching, hell isn't the place where you feel the torturous "final separation" from God. You will always be in His presence. Your reaction to the Son of God will determine if it's going to be an enjoyable presence or not.

If my child willingly and brutally paid with his life as a ransom for you and you still choose to deny him? Let's just say, you would not want to be in my presence ... my presence wouldn't feel like sunshine and rainbows.

Have you ever looked at coal? It's a dark substance; though light may shine on it, its nature refuses to reflect that light. When faced with fire, however, its darkness is not immune. The fire is all-consuming and the coal will eventually be transfigured from coal to fire. I believe that is how it will be in the afterlife. If you've denied Him (coal), you will in the end be confronted by the Fire.

Dualism would then mean that God (Father, Son, and Spirit) would be in an eternal war with another god. In our minds it would almost be a level playing field where they 'fight' for the souls of beings. WAIT! God is the only Uncreated Being and the accuser is created, just like you and me. He is a part of God's creation that went wrong, but he has no power outside of deception and blindness.

Of course, there are levels of blindness, but we won't go into that. Take some advice on this, please! I have been there, searching within the darkness to get knowledge of what is wrong and what is right. I've spent countless hours on YouTube and made myself an expert in the area of deception. Many Christians become obsessed with the devil; they are experts in darkness. Instead, we should continue to stay in the Light and we will find more of His Light. Looking for darkness is a sure way to get lost within darkness.

God is the source of all life and everyone needs this Life to live. "For as the Father has life in Himself, so He has granted the Son to have life in Himself" (John 5:26). This is a closed loop; God is the only source of life. Everything and everyone else will function from this Light.

You cannot look for the knowledge of darkness inside of darkness and come out reflecting more Light. Instead, you'll get stuck. "But if we walk in the light, as He is in the light, we have fellowship with one another, and the blood of Jesus, his Son, purifies us from all sin" (1 John 1:7). If we focus on His Light, we will be cleansed by this Light.

The first chapter of Colossians is perhaps one of my very favorites in scripture, and for good reason. In my earlier life, I didn't understand it fully; I was looking at it through a wrong frame. All my thoughts were still running through the filter of "God is for some and God is against some. God is in some and God is not in others. I'm in and you are out." God bless the church I attended as a child, but I knew that frame could not possibly be the gospel.

Let's look at Colossians 1:15-17 again.

> "The Son is the image of the invisible God, the firstborn over all creation. For in him **all** things were created: things in heaven and on earth, visible and invisible, whether thrones or powers or rulers or authorities; **all** things have been created through him and for him. He is before **all** things, and in him **all** things hold together."

I find these verses so powerful, breaking through any darkness planted by a dualistic mindset. Here are a couple of insights within these verses that have brought me comfort:

* The Son (The Word who became flesh) is the image of the invisible God. There is no difference between the two of them; they are the same. In the words of Jesus, *If you see me, you see the Father.* Jesus came to open eyes and show humanity who the Father is ... He is good. The ministry of Jesus revealed the character of the Father. They are One.

* For in Him all things were created. Paul makes sure he leaves nothing out. Heaven and earth, visible and invisible, rulers, principalities (angels)—*Everything* has been created *by Him* and *for Him.* He is before all things and inside of Him ALL are held together.

Read it again until it makes more sense.

If everything is inside of God, then nothing is outside of God. If anything could be outside of God (separated), it would need to be able to self-exist. Nothing self-exists except God alone. There is no other source of life but Him. If you believe that God could create and maintain outside of Himself, then you've started down the rabbit hole of dualism.

Ancient Greek philosophy claimed that "if" there is a god, it would be a deity watching us from afar. He would be a distant, holy god and would not be able to look at sin. He would be immovable and emotionless, after all, emotions are "moving", so a god must be free of such things. It also says that matter is fallen and goes to hell. The physical body with all its fleshly pleasures becomes the enemy in this philosophy. Therefore, we need to escape our bodies and become holy through certain steps.

Do you see how much philosophy has crept into Christianity? How could these philosophical tenets have become so intertwined with our Christian theology? Could this be the Christian God who became one of us? He supposedly can't look at sin, yet He became sin. He supposedly hates the physical body, yet he not only created it, He became flesh. He is supposedly distant, yet He calls us to be one with Him. He is supposedly emotionally unmoved, but it was love that moved Him to create us and to never forsake us.

"But those are all examples of Jesus", some may argue. The Lord our God is one God. The Father, Son, and Holy Spirit are one and the same. We don't have the Father not able to look at us, while Jesus became sin for us. We don't have the Father making us sick "to test our character", while Jesus heals our bodies and minds. Remember, Jesus said that He only does what He sees the Father do. Jesus healed as He saw the Father heal. Jesus comforted as He saw the Father comfort.

In sessions, I've found the following to be true. Some people are too ashamed to look at themselves and what they've done, so they try to hide the shame and not deal with it. In their fallen minds, they also believe that God can't look at it, because He can't look at sin. Who will help? They were looking at it from the wrong frame.

You can bring this to Him. He has been to the bottom of the darkness of humanity. He is not ashamed. He is not scared, and He is not taken aback. He is not surprised about anything. He does not condemn, nor does He accuse you. **Many may search for God, yet walk straight past Jesus, looking for the accuser.** The accuser of the brethren will accuse you day and night if you allow him. Our God lovingly leads us. Sometimes we lose our way, but He's got us.

Question:

1. What hidden shame or part of you would you like to give to Him?

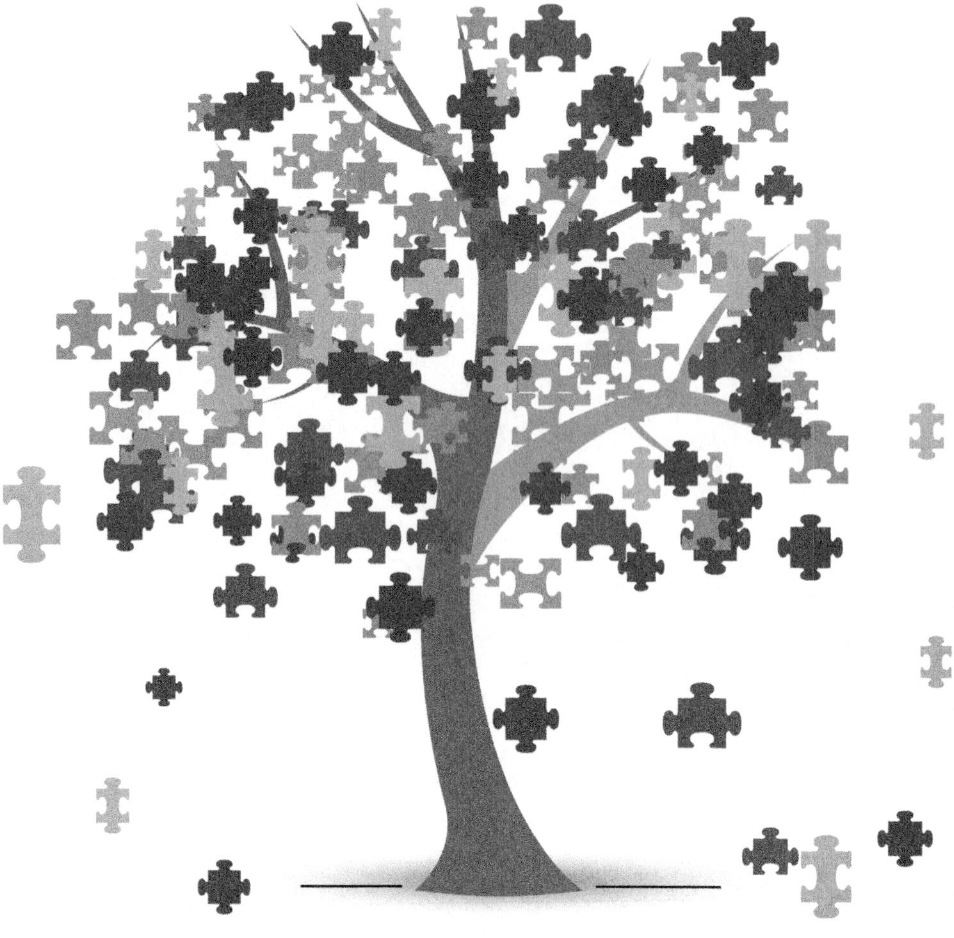

CHAPTER 12

The Puzzles of Our Life

"For many, the missing piece to the puzzle of life is the peace piece."

- Khang Kijarro Nguyen

One of my favorite things in the world is to watch human behavior. Since I was a small child, I've wanted to know what actually made people tick, why they would act a certain way. As clients sat in my office, they would tell me their life story. When it was my turn to speak, I'd start by asking them questions, trying to piece things together much like a jigsaw puzzle. Occasionally, I get the really big 5,000 piece puzzles who are difficult to solve. These clients tend to stay longer and see me more frequently. On the other hand, many times I get the 50 piece puzzle, and things come together very easily. Nonetheless, in each case I have to start with the corners as I work to the inside.

What about the puzzle of your life? Are you struggling with pieces that just don't want to fit? Maybe you have the wrong piece of the puzzle in your hand, but you don't even know it. Are you aware of what is going on in your life?

When you become aware of who you are deep down, and you're able to accept it, then you're able to help others in becoming aware of themselves and figuring out their own "puzzle pieces".

It doesn't matter who you are or where your morals or ethics or religion land. Inside all of us, there is a pain and a missing puzzle piece that we don't get. We have a yearning to be loved, to be home, to know where we are coming from and where we are going. This hole is deep and painful, and it bothers us. We can't fill it with anything from this earth. People will try with drugs, pornography, alcohol ... take your pick ... but you cannot fill it with anything except the knowledge of who Christ is, the One who takes our burdens.

When you live in awareness of who He is, you will begin conforming to Him, walking like Him, talking like Him. You will be aware of how you treat others, and you'll love them back to life.

EMOTIONAL IQ

What exactly is emotional IQ? Why is it so important? EI (emotional intelligence) is the ability to recognize your own emotions and those of others, and to use emotional information to guide their thoughts and behavior.

Methods of developing EI have become highly sought after by individuals who want to become more effective leaders. People can use EI to improve their mental health, reach their goals, and develop meaningful relationships.

Let me give you a few ways to improve your emotional intelligence:

PRACTICE OBSERVING HOW YOU FEEL.

Switch off your autopilot and switch on your awareness. We have busy lifestyles and it's all too easy to lose touch with your emotions. Slow down and reconnect with yourself. Choose a few different times during the day and set your watch. Take a deep breath and acknowledge how you feel.

TAKE TIME TO REFLECT ON YOUR OPINIONS.

Why do you believe what you believe? Is it because of what you were told? Look at the other side of the coin. Put yourself into someone else's shoes and try to walk in them. Take time and listen to the opinions of others. Everyone needs to be heard.

PAY ATTENTION TO YOUR WORDS, ACTIONS, AND BEHAVIORS.

While you are busy expanding your emotional awareness, also pay attention to your behavior. When you become aware of emotions during times of distress, it's easier to control them. You'll find a common thread in your emotional outbreaks.

TAKE RESPONSIBILITY FOR YOUR FEELINGS.

You are solely responsible for your own happiness, you cannot blame anyone else. Your emotions and behavior belong to you, no one else.

UNDERSTAND YOUR MOTIVATION.

What motivates you? What excites you? Whatever you do in life, always remember the reason you are doing it in the first place. Whether it's a project, or moving to a different continent, be honest with yourself about your motives. When you begin questioning whether you should stay where you are, you can remind yourself why you are doing it in the first place.

ACKNOWLEDGE YOUR EMOTIONAL TRIGGERS.

Individuals who are self-aware are able to recognize their emotions as they occur. Take time to process your emotions before you communicate them.

HAVE EMPATHY.

Before you're able to empathize with anyone, you must listen. Try to really understand what they are saying. Let them talk without interruption, without judgment, and without criticism. It's important for everyone to be heard. Listen to them, absorb their situation, and consider how they are feeling before you react.

MANAGE YOUR NEGATIVE EMOTIONS.

When you learn to manage your negative emotions, you get less overwhelmed in negative situations. How do you manage your negative emotions? Don't jump to conclusions, see the situation from another angle, and put yourself in the shoes of the person with whom you're getting upset.

BE TRANSPARENT.

No one has had the perfect life, and being transparent and opening up to someone shows your humility and willingness to be vulnerable. Give me someone who is real, who has made mistakes and is still willing to face life with courage, and we'll be friends for a very long time!

PURSUE COMPASSION ON YOURSELF AND OTHERS

"Love one another; as I have loved you" (John 13:34). That's quite a tall order, Jesus, but we will try!

Humor me. If it is true that Christ is in all, (not just the Jews, or those who believe, repent, and get baptized) then all of humanity sits with a problem. We have been living in our dualistic bubble, unaware of how big He really is. If Christ tells me to love my enemy and He is in my enemy, too, upholding them and sustaining them … it means that when I hate my enemy, I am hostile towards Christ. When I slander my enemy, I am also bad mouthing Jesus inside of my enemy.

"Then the King will say to those on his right, 'Come, you who are blessed by my Father; take your inheritance, the kingdom prepared for you since the creation of the world. For I was hungry and you gave me something to eat, I was thirsty and you gave me something to drink, I was a stranger and you invited me in, I needed clothes and you clothed me, I was sick and you looked after me, I was in prison and you came to visit me.'

Then the righteous will answer him, 'Lord, when did we see you hungry and feed you, or thirsty and give you something to drink? When did we see you a stranger and invite you in, or needing clothes and clothe you? When did we see you sick or in prison and go to visit you?' The King will reply, 'Truly I tell you, whatever you did for one of the least of these brothers and sisters of mine, you did for me.'

Then he will say to those on his left, 'Depart from me, you who are cursed, into the eternal fire prepared for the devil and his angels. For I was hungry and you gave me nothing to eat, I was thirsty and you gave me nothing to drink, I was a stranger and you did not invite me in, I needed clothes and you did not clothe me, I was sick and in prison and you did not look after me.'
They also will answer, 'Lord, when did we see you hungry or thirsty or a stranger or needing clothes or sick or in prison, and did not help you?' He will reply, 'Truly I tell you, whatever you did not do for one of the least of these, you did not do for me." (Matthew 25:34-45).

With this in mind, you should look for Christ in people. You'll be surprised how things change when you search for Him in people that you'd otherwise rather ignore. Start noticing other people's problems; care for what they are going through.

If we really look at what Jesus is asking, to love like He loves ... are there any conditions? No, it's unconditional. Have compassion for the mistakes you make; you are only human. I am no better than you; I just have different sin. There is no sliding scale. Just as you learn how to have compassion toward others, you can begin to have compassion toward yourself.

PUT YOUR THOUGHTS ON TRIAL

As humans, we can be so hard on ourselves. Our thought life can feel like we are constantly on trial, and we tend to be on the losing side. Instead of being in the "hot seat", position yourself in the mercy seat and reverse the trial. In other words, put your thoughts on trial.

You can't control the thoughts that come into your mind, but you can control what you focus on (meditate on), and how you respond to those thoughts. You are not your thoughts, so don't beat yourself up.

As previously discussed, your body will have a physical response to your thoughts. Whether they are good, healthy thoughts or unhealthy, toxic thoughts, they will both trigger a reaction in your body. What you need to do is discern the wise, healthy thoughts, and a tool to sharpen this discernment is to put your thoughts on trial.

Although it can seem that our negative thoughts are naturally a part of how our mind works, we have a choice to focus on the thoughts we want and to ignore the ones which hurt, upset, or destroy us. Ever heard the saying "a wandering mind is an unhappy mind"? Well, now you have! **When you let your thoughts run free, they will probably end up at the last place you want them to be.**

Let's say the voice in your head tells you that you're not good enough for the job for which you're applying. It's the morning of the interview and you begin doubting yourself. You may feel sick to your stomach and your heart may race, but during these moments of physical distress, it's your mind that needs your focus. By monitoring and changing your thought process, you alter how your body is responding. What you should do is use your free will (remember lesson 1) to validate and focus on the thoughts which will deliver the emotional consequence and reaction you want to occur. Again, how do you take control of your life? By self-regulating your thoughts!

I am going to show you how you take control. Consider a particularly unhelpful thought you've had in the past and write it in the space below. Placing this thought on trial can often help to change it, which in turn helps us to change how we feel.

Assess the thought and answer these questions honestly. (This is all about self awareness.)

1. What is the thought you'd like to place on trial?

2. What is your evidence that supports this thought?

3. What is your evidence contrary to the thought?

4. Have you looked at this thought from all angles?

5. Is it possible that you may have limited evidence and may not see the big picture?

6. What would your best friend say about this?

7. Would this matter a year from now? Five years from now? What about ten years from now?

Once you have asked yourself these questions, read through your answers and try to come up with a more balanced or rational view. In the future, try to apply these questions to any unhelpful thoughts that are revealed. You can use this technique to test whether or not your thoughts are realistic and balanced and to better manage your thought life.

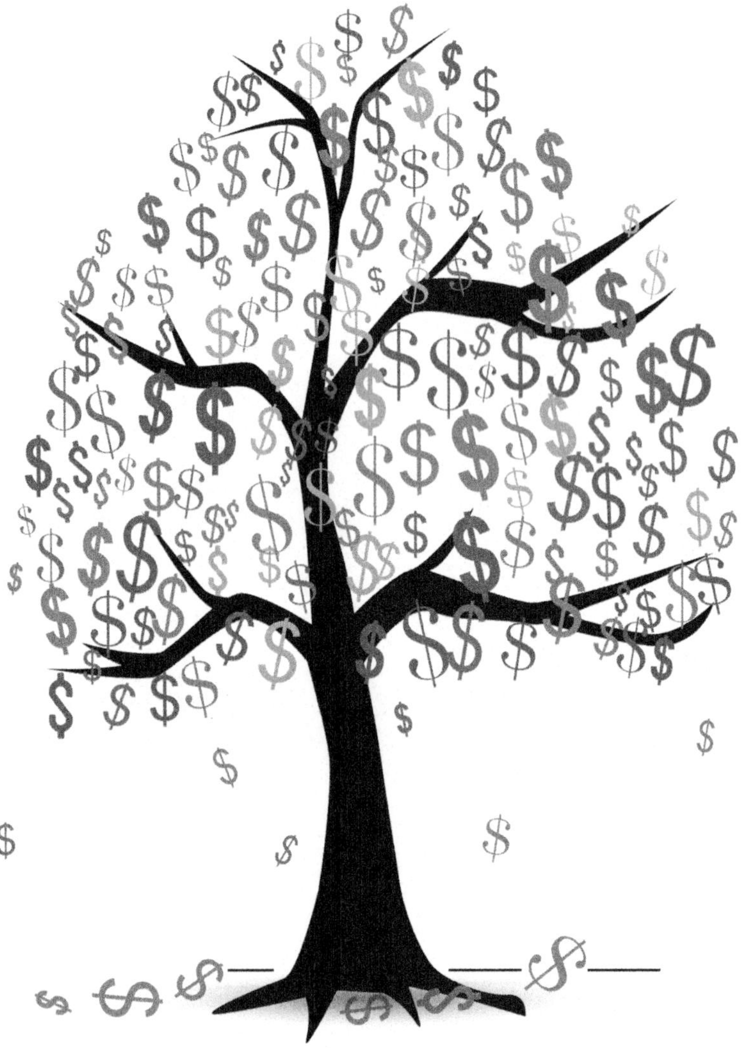

CHAPTER 13

Anxiety

"Be anxious for nothing, but in everything by prayer and supplication, with thanksgiving, let your requests be made known to God; and the peace of God, which surpasses all understanding, will guard your hearts and minds through Christ Jesus."

(Philippians 4:6-7)

Sebastian has OCD (Obsessive-Compulsive Disorder) and it drives him insane. He can't stop the OCD, but this stems from anxiety. He just hates what he is doing and he tells me every session how he wishes he could stop. He has debilitating anxiety up to the point that he struggles to breathe, and many times can't even hear what I am saying. He can't sit still, so often paces up and down. Eventually he sits down, then starts rocking. He tells me that he wants nothing to do with science, since he believes it's from the devil. He also wants to stop his anxiety medication, because it's an idol in God's eyes.

Note: My first go-to is to challenge irrational thoughts and that will typically lead me to his core belief.

"Why do you believe it's an idol? Who told you that?" I asked.

"The Bible said I should not put anything before God" he answered.

"Do you love your medication more than you love God?" I asked.

"No," he said. "<u>I just want to please God and for Him to be happy with me and become One with me.</u>"

So, what core belief did he just reveal? He believes God is not pleased with him and that he needs to change in order to be accepted. Our conversation continues.

"Ok,' I said. 'If you stop your medication, you might as well stop eating and drinking. You might have to stop spending time with friends who support you. Sometimes I need to sleep for a day just to cope with life with everything that's going on. Do you feel I need to stop sleeping? What do you think?" (*We can use hundreds of examples here.*)

... pause ...

"So, do you still think your medication is an idol?" I finally ask.

Sebastian thinks. "Is the body not fallen?"

"Why do you ask?" I replied.

"Someone told me," he said.

"Are they an expert in this field?" I asked him.

"No."

I could see him processing his thoughts, so I waited a moment before I answered, "Jesus became flesh for us, Sebastian, so that argument doesn't hold water. He took your flesh and cleaned it up. The body cannot be fallen."

Again we go into the teachings of dualism, dividing things. In this case, Sebastian had divided body and spirit.

P.S. I love how Jesus would always answer a question with another question.

THINK.

Sebastian is in thought, and I notice that he's stopped rocking and calmed down. He stopped fidgeting and he is rationally thinking about things.

"What if the thought of you needing to change in order to be accepted is really making you anxious and is the trigger to your panic?" I asked him. I then proceeded to offer him a couple different scenarios. "Just to try and organize your thoughts, I want you to tell me what your reaction is to my questions, rating your anxiety level from 1-10."

"Scenario 1," I start. "You use medication and, therefore, it's your idol. God is angry and will punish you somehow for using it. He will turn His back on you until you can change."

I then asked him to gauge his level of anxiety.

"Fifteen!" he exclaimed. "It's through the roof!"

Next I layed out Scenario 2:

"God is holding you together through the mess and the torment. He has seen what you have been through, and He has never left you, nor forsaken you. He knows how you are wired, and He loves you. He is walking with you until you are healed. Picture the everlasting arms."

Again, I asked him to gauge his level of anxiety.

His answer?

"... NONE."

Which is the healthier thought and why? Have you ever heard the saying *what you fear, you create*? What if the very thing you're afraid of is shaping your reality and enforcing your core values?

Cognitive behavioral therapy (CBT) has become the leading treatment for anxiety, and for good reason. CBT works by identifying and addressing how a person's thoughts and behaviors interact to create anxiety. An emotion like anxiety is very hard to change, so you need to target the thought that leads to the undesired emotion.

Let's look at the following example. This is a situation that needs to be interpreted.

SITUATION: You are required to give a presentation in front of board members.

REACTION A:

Thought	Emotion	Behavior
I'll practice and do great!	Confident Anticipatory	Practices and completes the presentation without a problem.

REACTION B:

Thought	Emotion	Behavior
I bet I make a fool of myself in front of everyone!	Anxious Worried Scared	Puts off practicing. Attempts to get out of doing the presentation.

In the first chapter, I spoke about the brain and our thought processes. For every thought you have, there is a physical reaction in your body. If you were to focus and meditate on the thought that you will make a fool of yourself, your brain will release chemicals which will either be in insufficient or excessive amounts, which in turn will have a negative effect on your body.

I want you to start focusing on the thoughts that contribute to your anxiety, and one of the best ways to do this is by a Thought Log. (Yes, I send clients home with homework.) A Thought Log will require you to describe situations that you experience, record the thought you had during that situation, and then the resulting consequence (both a behavior and emotion). Without practice in identifying how thoughts and emotions are linked, the most important thoughts will pass by unnoticed and unchallenged.

Let look at the example again:

SITUATION: You are required to give a presentation in front of board members.

Challenge	Consequence
Although this is scary, I've never messed up before. Even if I make a fool of myself, it will all be forgotten in a week. What is the worst thing that can happen?	You're nervous, but not to such a debilitating level. You follow through with the presentation. Now the next time will be easier!

I invite you to play this script till the end:

Q: What is the worst thing that can happen?
A: I'll make a fool of myself.
Q: What is the worst thing that can happen if you make a fool out of yourself?
A: My colleagues will laugh.
Q: What is the worst thing if your colleagues laugh?
A: I'll feel silly.
Q: What is the worst thing about feeling silly?
A: ... hmmm ...

Another great tool I use with anxiety:

If you have a certain thought that gives you panic and anxiety, I want you to do the following. I want you to discern if you think this is a rational thought or irrational thought. Measure the level of anxiety this thought gives you from 1 to 10. (1 being not stressed at all to 10 being climbing out the walls here!) Keep asking the questions. Play the script till the end. What is the worst thing that can happen? When you see it for what it is—that there is nothing to fear—then measure the level of anxiety you have again. You'll find that the number went down drastically.

Here is a blank Thought Log where you can record your thought, challenge, and consequence:

Thought Log

Situation:

Thought:

Challenge:

Consequence:

_____
_____
_____
_____
_____

ANXIETY EDUCATION

Do you actually know why you are scared of certain things? Can you pinpoint it? Why do they make you anxious? Are you anxious about things that are totally out of your control?

You might know that you are afraid of snakes, social events, or cars, but that's about it. Others might have a constant feeling of anxiety without really knowing what it's about. It's a good idea to start discussing triggers, or your source of anxiety. What are the situations when you feel most anxious? What physically happens in your body? How is it affecting your life and the lives of your loved ones?

If you have been able to pinpoint that thought, I want you to look at some points regarding this thought:

> Do you have any evidence to support this thought?
>
> What would your best friend say about this thought?
>
> Will this matter in 1 year, 5 years, or 10 years from now?
>
> What would most likely happen? Could it be that you have a distorted thinking pattern? (Ex: Catastrophizing—always assuming the worst.)

RELAXATION SKILLS

With CBT, therapists intervene by changing negative thought patterns and behaviors which would worsen the problem. Relaxation skills are also an important aspect in this teaching.

Breath of Life: Your breath is the only thing you always take with you. You might move continents, you'll lose people you love, you'll feel betrayed, you'll get anxious ... you will go through emotions. What is the one thing that changes when your emotions change? Your breathing. What happens when we have a fright, or get angry or sad? Our breathing changes. The next technique will be focused on your breathing. When you start with deep breathing, you become conscious of what you are doing . You will learn to breathe slowly using your diaphragm to initiate the body's relaxation response.

Instructions: Deep Breathing

1. Sit comfortably in your chair. Place your hand on your stomach so you are able to feel your diaphragm move as you breathe.

2. Take a deep breath through your nose. Breathe in slowly. Time the breath to last 5 seconds.

3. Hold each breath for 5 seconds. You can do less time if it's difficult or uncomfortable.

4. Release the air slowly (again, time 5 seconds). Do this by puckering your lips and pretending that you are blowing through a straw (it can be helpful to actually use a straw for practice).

5. Repeat this process for about 5 minutes, preferably three times a day. The more you practice, the more effective deep breathing will be when you need it.

Deep breathing can be valuable in the moment when confronting something anxiety-producing, or in general as a way to reduce overall stress. It also gives your body a way to counteract the rush of adrenaline produced.

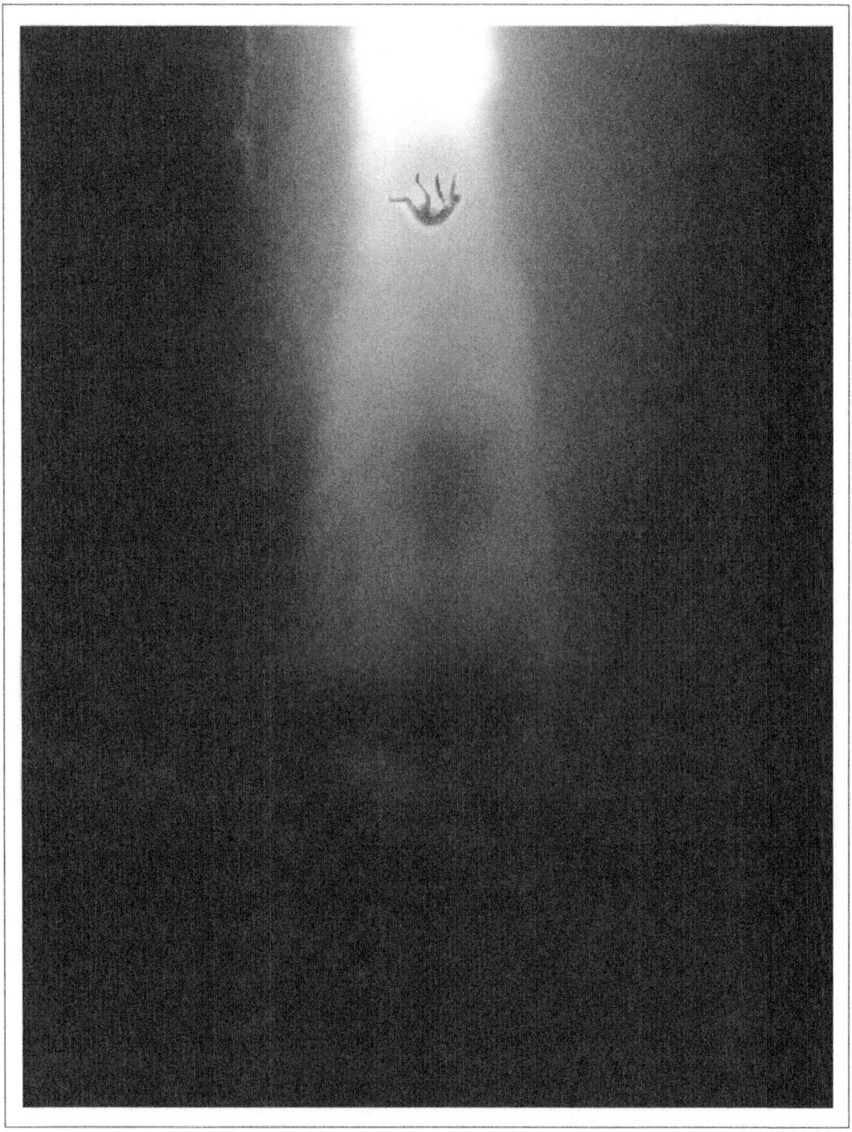

CHAPTER 14

Hopelessness

"Hope deferred makes the heart sick, But when the desire comes, it is a tree of life."

(Proverbs 13:12)

You know that feeling when even just getting out of bed is too much. This is very common with people living with depression. They feel completely out of hope. Even if you don't have depression, I am sure you've come across this debilitating emotion.

To have this emotion coupled with depression can feel like it's sucking the life right out of you. Unfortunately, hopelessness is a primary contributing factor in the development of suicidal thinking and behaviors, so I urge you to get in contact with a counselor if you have suicidal ideation.

Hopelessness is the consequence of seeing no solutions to problems and the activation of beliefs related to negative expectations, for example: *I can never be happy, I am a freak,* or *I am a burden to my family and they will be better without me.*

Hopelessness is more strongly related to suicide intent than depression is, because it seems there is no way out. My immediate goal in addressing hopelessness is to challenge the belief that your situation cannot get better. You may overestimate the magnitude of your problem and underestimate the available resources. It is important to see if this is a distorted belief system, and you do that by looking at the evidence that contradicts that belief. Now, I may be repeating certain things over and over, but rest assured that I do this with a goal in mind.

Are you confusing a thought with a fact? Just because you believe it, does it make it true?

Do you have evidence that this situation will not change?

Can you present me with the evidence?

Is it possible that you are jumping to conclusions?

Is this "all or nothing" thinking?

Are you catastrophizing - always expecting the worst possible outcome?

What alternatives do you have?

Are you feeling shame or condemnation in any way?

Are you concentrating on your weaknesses and forgetting your strengths?

What are your strengths?

An emotion like hopelessness is very difficult to change, so let's start talking about the thoughts that enable you to feel hopeless. I want to target your thoughts in order to change your emotion. Negative thinking can slow down depression recovery, that's why it's so important to take thoughts captive.

Research has made a surprising observation: people with depression don't lack positive emotions, they just don't allow themselves to feel them. This is called dampening. It suppresses positive emotions with distortions like:

> I don't deserve this.

> I am never going to be happy.

> Nobody likes me.

> It's never going to get better.

One of the best tools to counteract the dampening effect is journaling. It recalibrates the part of your brain that has a firm grip on happy thoughts. For every negative thought, there is a healthy positive one. Opt for the latter.

Dampening Effect: In short, it's like a child holding onto their toys, not wanting to share. Your brain is the friend wanting to share and journaling is the 'psychologist' sitting down with the child explaining why they need to share.

Here are more tools to help you when you're feeling hopeless:

Express Yourself: Many of the drawings you see in this book are made by clients who need to express themselves, so I ask them to draw. The drawings are deep and help them cope with certain situations in their life. Write poetry, work on a painting, or sculpt clay. It'll all help you change your outlook on life in a positive way.

Volunteer: Do good to others by volunteering somewhere that there's a cause you support. Whether it's at a soup kitchen or at the SPCA, we are all family and we should look after each other. Helping those less fortunate will help you look at your own life in a more positive way.

Join a Like-Minded Group: We are meant to be in a community, and we heal in relationships with others. We learn from each other, we bounce ideas off each other, and we confide in those we trust. As humans, it's of the utmost importance that we stay connected.

Scripture Meditation: This is where you need to feed your mind with encouragement. Meditate on the promises God gave you. Here is an encouraging verse from Jeremiah 29:11. "For I know the thoughts that I think toward you, says the Lord, thoughts of peace and not of evil, to give you a future and a hope." God's thoughts for you are filled with peace; He isn't frustrated with you. His plans for your future are filled with hope; He hasn't given up on you!

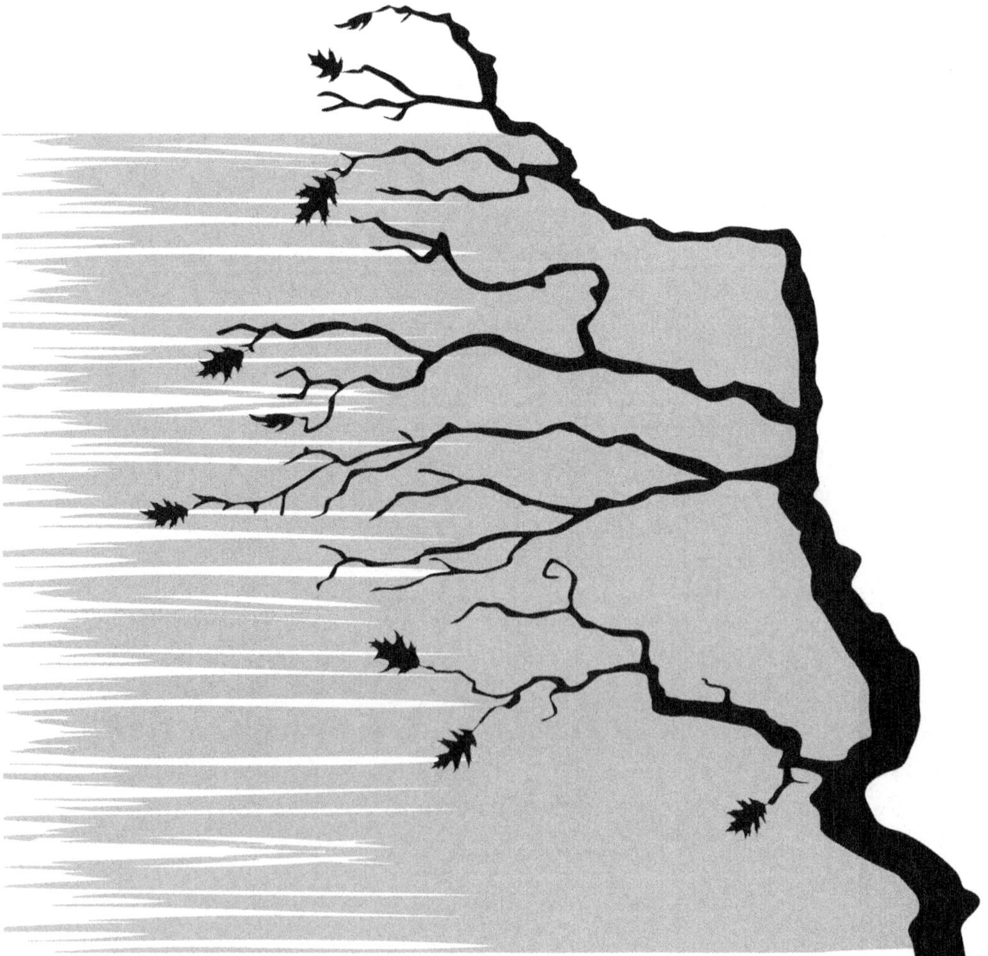

CHAPTER 15

Anger Management

> *"'I lose my temper, but it's all over in a minute,' said the student. 'So is the hydrogen bomb,' I replied. 'But think of the damage it produces!'"*
>
> George Sweeting

Anger is much more common than you think. People will come to see me regularly because of their anger. "It's like I just tap out," they say.

Danny is a gentleman who came to see me quite regularly. He grew up in a dysfunctional home and told me he does not fit in. He said that people irritate him and make him angry. I heard that he once tried to strangle someone in anger, simply because things didn't go his way. He was always on the edge, always ready to fight. So here he was sitting in a room with me, a situation he really did not want to be in. Nonetheless, an ultimatum had been set for him, so there we were.

Danny became extremely angry at times, but anger is an emotion and emotions are very hard to change. It doesn't do much good to simply tell someone that they shouldn't get so angry. Rather, one has to search through the minefield of thoughts that tend to trigger that emotion. What are you thinking of when you get angry like this?

We can't control what thoughts enter our mind, but we can choose to act upon them or not. All people have the ability to choose a new set of habits, thought patterns, and behavior. It's not people who disturb us, it's our thoughts and perceptions about people. You can choose to act on it or not.

One of the best cognitive tools I've given people with this problem is the "Stop Sign Approach". This takes some practice, but if you master this, you'll thank me.

1. Take the thought captive.

    You need to detect it early, so when you get that first trigger, I want you to take that thought captive under the obedience of Christ. Where is this coming from? Who is the source? Is this a lie that I am believing?

2. Stop Sign Approach.

    When you start feeling that rush of emotions enter your mind, I want you to imagine a stop sign—a big, red stop sign!

    Tell yourself to stop!
    Imagine the stop sign 30 meters from you.

    Tell yourself to stop!
    Imagine the stop sign 15 meters from you.

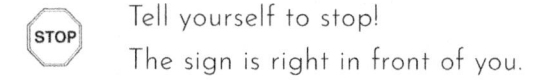

    Tell yourself to stop!
    The sign is right in front of you.

    Breathe ... and tell yourself to stop. Tell your body to stop. This way you train your brain to cognitively think and become aware that you are in control. Also, when people experience anger, they not only experience it emotionally, but physically as well. Adrenaline is pumped into the body, which creates the physical urge to react. Train yourself to STOP, so that you can recognize and adjust to the adrenaline rush, and allow yourself time to process mentally.

3. Catch the Warning Signs.

   Sometimes anger can make you do things before you even recognize what you're doing or how you are feeling. You may constantly live in anger. When this is the case, it may not feel like anger ... it feels normal. Your body has grown accustomed to the chemicals released during these outbursts and you may not even notice it. It's like hearing the sound of an airplane takeoff when you work at the airport, or the sound of an air conditioner in a room—your mind will start blocking it. Even if you're not aware of your anger, it still influences your behavior.

   The first step in managing anger is to "catch" the first warning signs, and they may differ from person to person. How do you react when you are angry? You can check the warning sign:

   o   I start sweating.

   o   I zone out.

   o   I start breathing fast.

   o   I stare at the other person aggressively.

   o   My body becomes rigid.

   o   My face becomes hot and flustered.

   o   My mind goes blank.

   o   Other: _____

   When you don't recognize these triggers, you may begin screaming or yelling, or saying things that you did not want to say. You may punch walls or doors, or throw things. You may become aggressive, argumentative, or you may begin to cry.

Here is a list of skills and tools to help manage anger:

Recognize early warning signs, as discussed above.

Take a Time-Out. Temporarily leave the situation that is making you angry. It won't solve the problem, but it will give you time to re-organize your thoughts and calm down.

Breathe. Start breathing. Count as you breathe in and count as you breathe out. It will take your mind off things, if nothing else.

Exercise. Not only is this good for your physical health, this is good for your mental health, too. Your brain will release "feel good" hormones, creating a sense of relaxation and warmth.

Think of the Consequences. What will the outcome be? Will arguing help you? Will this matter one year from now? Will it matter five years from now? What about ten years from now? If it won't matter, think about whether it's worth arguing over.

Question:

1. What angers you?

2. What can you do next time to better the situation?

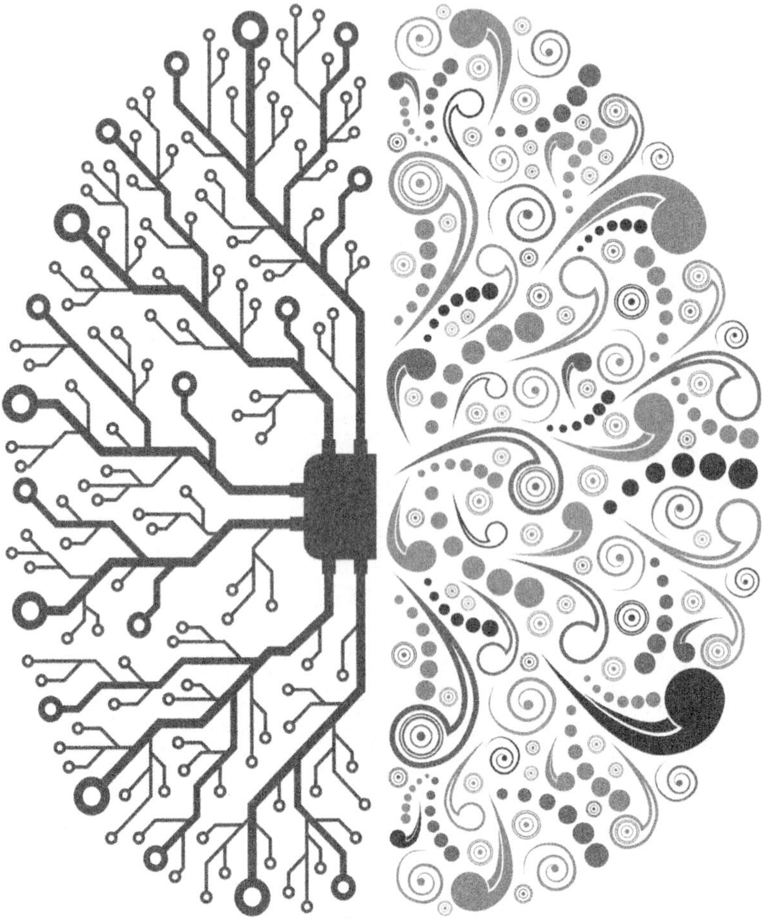

CHAPTER 16

Obsessive Compulsive Disorder

"It's like you have two brains — a rational brain and an irrational brain. And they're constantly fighting."

Emilie Ford.

"These rituals make me insane! Please help me! I have to do these darn rituals every day and I can't stop doing it. I have to wake up at 8:03, take my medication, and get back into bed. I then have to pray until 9:00 just to get through the morning. It petrifies me. My thoughts seem like they are making me crazy. I can't help myself."

People with OCD are distressed over their thoughts or obsessions, because they interpret them as warnings of events that are dangerous and likely to occur, when in fact they seem to be irrational. I would like to help you identify these automatic unrealistic thoughts and change your interpretation of the meaning of the thoughts, resulting in decreased anxiety and decreased compulsions.

It's all about awareness. After you are aware of the obsession, we can tackle the problem. You need to keep a daily diary of obsessions which is called a Thought Log. In the Thought Log, you should write down your obsessions and the interpretations associated with the obsessions. Important details to record may include what you were doing when the obsession began, the content of the obsession, the meaning attributed to the obsession, and what you did in response to the obsession (usually a compulsion).

I would like you to stand outside of the situation and look at it through the eyes of a bystander. Then I would like you to use gentle reasoning to see if this is in fact a rational thought or an irrational thought. Let's challenge your belief. This will better equip you to discern whether it's a healthy or unhealthy thought. Knowing that beliefs start off with a thought, let's look at the thought. We can do this through Socratic questioning.

Socratic Questioning:

1. Thought to be challenged:

2. What is the evidence for your thought?

3. What is the evidence against your thought?

4. Who is in control of this thought?

5. Are you basing this thought on facts or feelings?

6. Could you be misinterpreting the evidence?

7. Are you making any assumptions? What are they?

8. Are you having this thought out of habit?

9. Did someone pass this thought to you? Are they a reliable source?

10. Is your thought a likely scenario, or is it the worst-case scenario?

Once you are able to quickly identify your obsessions and compulsions as symptoms of OCD, there are behavioral experiments such as Exposure Therapy to disprove errors in thinking about cause and effect. While avoidance of fearful situations may feel better for the short term, that fear is only allowed to take deeper root. Exposure Therapy uses a safe environment to face the fear and in turn create a platform of experience to support rational thought.[1] There's power in knowing something from experience. To face a fear and come out safely makes it easier to believe that can happen again.

For example, Andrew could never leave his house. He believed that he would be injured if he left. I first challenged him on this thought with a simple question: Why do you believe that? I then began *challenging* him. The first week, I had him walk 200 meters outside to the first building. The next week, I had him walk 600 meters outside. Now he is walking 10 km per day. He also believed he needed to eat at 12:00 noon, exactly, everyday. Instead of catering to this felt need, I challenged him to eat at a later time.

I use his experiment as material for discussion on irrational behavior. Once you are outside of this scenario, you are able to see clearly. Over time, you will learn to identify and re-evaluate beliefs about the potential consequences of engaging in or refraining from compulsive behaviors and, subsequently, begin to eliminate compulsions.

According to science, there is no cure for OCD. However, I lean to the fact that OCD stems from anxiety. If you get your anxiety under control, your OCD will only benefit from it! I boldly say this, because I have seen how some people's OCD habits disappear when they are in a calm, loving environment where they are treated with love and understanding.

COGNITIVE REFRAMING

Reframing is changing the way you look at things and, therefore, changing your experience of the situation. If you are living in a stressful situation, or perceive that you are in a stressful situation, your fight-or-flight response will kick in. Many clients will come see me due to a constant sense of hyper-vigilance and perceiving threats when there are none. You'll find that your body will go into fight-or-flight with no trigger, merely because your body is always on high alert. How can you break free of this feeling?

START REFRAMING YOUR THOUGHTS:

Being aware of your thoughts is an important part in challenging and ultimately changing your thinking. One thing you can do is become an observer—look from the outside in. You should write down your observations in order to look at them at a later stage. Note your thoughts, as well as how you interpreted the situation.

Here's an example of looking at a situation as though you were merely a bystander, an observer: You forgot to call a friend on her birthday. Now, you've been trying to reach her, but she doesn't answer the phone. Immediately you start wondering, *Is she mad at me? How long will she keep ignoring me? Will she ever forgive me? Am I losing my friend?* See how this inner dialogue plays off in your mind? Also, note the physical response it has in your body. Sadness, regret, and anger may be some of the emotions you feel. If you were the bystander to this situation, would you be able to offer some other possibilities of why the friend isn't answering her phone? Would you be able to offer some healthy perspective? As it turns out, the friend had simply left her phone at home, wanting a relaxing day without disturbance. She is not even aware that you called, but she would love to speak to you.

When situations such as this one arise, try to mentally remove yourself from it in order to gain an observer's perspective.

Question:

1. For practice, can you think of more examples where you could have been wrong about a certain situation?

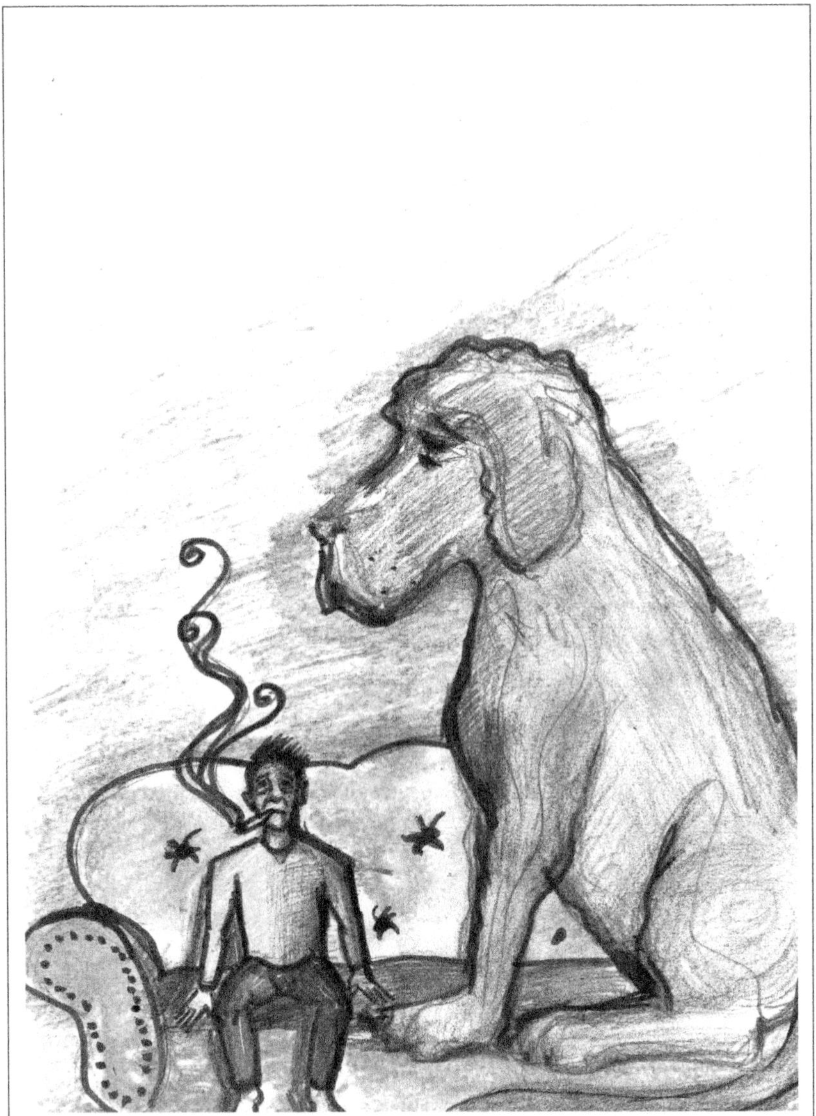

CHAPTER 17

Depression: The Big Black Dog

"Depression is a prison where you are both the suffering prisoner and the cruel jailer."

Dorothy Rowe

The Big Black Dog ... go ahead and google it.[1] Whenever he appears, life seems empty and meaningless. Sometimes he would show up without warning, and out of the blue make you wonder what the purpose of life is. You may look at people surrounding you, how they enjoy life, how they laugh and love, yet you feel all alone. It doesn't matter how far you try to walk away from the dog, he relentlessly follows you. It doesn't matter where you try to hide, when you look up ... there he is. He ruins your appetite for life and takes the joy out of anything that means something to you.

Honestly, the older you get, the more the black dog hangs around. He gets bigger with time and starts to take over your life, nearly smothering you. You may begin medicating yourself, hoping to stop seeing the dog for just a few days. Yet, there he remains.

Millions of people all over the world struggle with this dog, it is nothing to be ashamed of. The more tired you are, the more he sticks around. The more stressed you are, the closer he'll get.

Become aware of yourself, your thoughts, and your triggers. Speak to a professional who can help you get the dog under control. The more aware you are of yourself and who you are, the less persistent the mutt will be. He may never go completely, but through the right exercises, you can teach him some manners. Sit. Wait. Rollover. You can master him.

There are several studies that show cognitive psychotherapy of depression is at least as effective, if not more effective, than drugs for the treatment of mildly and moderately severe depression. These studies go back to one reported by the founder of cognitive therapy, Aaron Beck, twenty years ago.[2] If medication is not working for you, CBT might.

Honestly speaking, there seems to be a dark hole in all of humanity. I have a hypothesis about this hole ... humor me. We came from God, who is Spirit. We are flesh, and even though we have the Spirit, we yearn for Him like a child for his mother. You can try to medicate the child in order to lessen the pain, but it doesn't work. This pain clearly can't be medicated with anything from this world. The best thing to do is this: be aware of the hole. Look at it (metaphorically speaking).

If you look down that deep, dark hole, you will see Who is standing at the bottom. It's Jesus, the Everlasting Arms, the Tree of Life running through all of creation, the Great I Am. When you can't cope with life, when you are kicking and screaming, and asking where He is in the midst of your pain ... He's right there, holding you together when you feel like falling apart.

> "The eternal God is your refuge, and underneath are the everlasting arms."
>
> (Deuteronomy 33:27)

Cognitive behavior therapy takes a different approach to an emotion like depression. It has little, if any, interest in the past or in the reasons you became depressed. Rather, the whole focus of the treatment is on the irrational, unrealistic beliefs that *keep* you depressed. You may have the belief that you are a freak, or that you are overweight and unlovable, or that only by losing weight could you ever be loved by someone. To deal with these beliefs, I would expand on the reasons why you believe them.

This brings me back to dealing with cognitive distortion: Who told you that? Are they an expert in the field? What is your evidence for what you are saying? Could it be that you are wrong? If you have been stuck in an unhelpful way of thinking for most of your life, you will know what kind of abuse you go through by mentally believing this. The only way to break an abusive cycle is to go the other way. In plain terms, if your brain has been used to doing something for so long, it becomes automatic. Through this book you have, hopefully, realized that you can be intentional about changing your thought processes, growing healthy "neuro-trees" that recalibrate your whole self. You can live victorious!

I have a client who lives in Canada. He has complex OCD, social anxiety, suicidal ideation, depression ... he came to me without any hope. He had been released from a mental institution, though they told him that he would probably end up there again. Thus, he lived in fear that the institution was his inevitable destination. After a month of counseling, he warmed up a bit. After two months, he was in a much better place. He met someone, and he was laughing for the first time in years.

It all started by pushing him to do small steps ... walk to the first tree outside your house and bring a leaf back. The next day, walk a bit farther. Then go farther, because you can! You are not limited, and His plan is for you to prosper. Trust me! This gentleman still has OCD. We "have to" talk at a specific time. But if we don't? (You know the drill by now.) What is the worst thing that can happen?

Cognitive therapy challenges these clearly counterfactual beliefs, some of them self-accusatory, some of them unreasonable, unfulfillable expectations. Effective tools are confrontation, demonstration (of irrationality), and re-education. Cognitive therapy expands the depressed person's experience of the possible. It is all about getting out of the self-imposed trap that constrictive, distorted thinking imposes. I would begin pushing people, lovingly, towards freedom. Your whole being will shout "no!", but if you take small steps, it leads to freedom and liberty.

People usually turn to me if they have gone through all the avenues and there is nothing they can do anymore. I wanted to be a lawyer growing up, I could argue about *anything* and it'll be airtight! From a young age, I could not tolerate bullies, and to this day I am fiercely protective over anyone needing my help. Today, I still argue, but I limit the arguments to irrational thoughts, accusations, unfairness, and distortions. I bring them to the Light of Christ. Now, you go ahead and bring each of these to the Light so that you can see it for what it is.

Right now, for those who are chronically depressed, I want to challenge the belief that things are hopeless, that the only light at the end of the tunnel is the impending locomotive. On the contrary, there's a possibility that although the depression has been a blinder, despite all the torment that's been endured, it's still possible to see the Light. His Light can shine through any darkness.

I remember preaching at a church not too long ago. A woman came up to me after the service, and I asked her what I could help her with and whether I could pray for her. She looked up at me and said, "I just want to die. Please help me." There was not really a lot of time, and people were waiting for me. I placed my hands on her and asked God to open her eyes to see where He was.

On that Monday, I received a message from her:

"I have seen psychologists all my life, and I see a psychiatrist once a week. I planned my suicide. I bought a dress for my daughter for the funeral. I had decided where I would go in order to end it. But when you laid hands on me, a dark mass just lifted off me and I could see ... I have never been alone; He is always with me. I am quite ashamed of my thoughts, and I don't know what you did, but I have no intention of dying anymore. He has given me my life back."

I still see her regularly, once every two weeks ... but we go for coffee and carrot cake. We laugh and make silly jokes. We share in the love and the relationship He planted in us all.

As a refresher, CBT model works on the following premise:

An emotion (like depression, often stemming from hopelessness) is difficult to change directly, so CBT targets emotions by intervening in thoughts and behaviors that are contributing to the distressing emotions. It is crucial that we challenge any thoughts that cause us harm.

Consider a recurring negative thought that you're currently experiencing in life. Then take a few minutes to answer each of the following questions, and record thorough responses. Elaborate, and explain 'why' or 'why not' in each answer.

1. What is the evidence for your thought?

_____

_____

_____

_____

2. What is the evidence *against* your thought?

_____

_____

_____

_____

3. Who is in control of this thought?

_____

_____

_____

_____

4. Are you basing this thought on facts or feelings?

5. Could you be misinterpreting the evidence?

6. Are you making any assumptions? What are they?

7. Might other people have different interpretations of the same situation? What are they?

8. Are you looking at all the evidence or just that which supports your thought?

9. Are you looking at it from all angles?

10. Is your thought a likely scenario, or is it the worst-case scenario?

11. What would a friend think about the thought?

12. What would a judge think about it?

13. What would Jesus think about the thought?

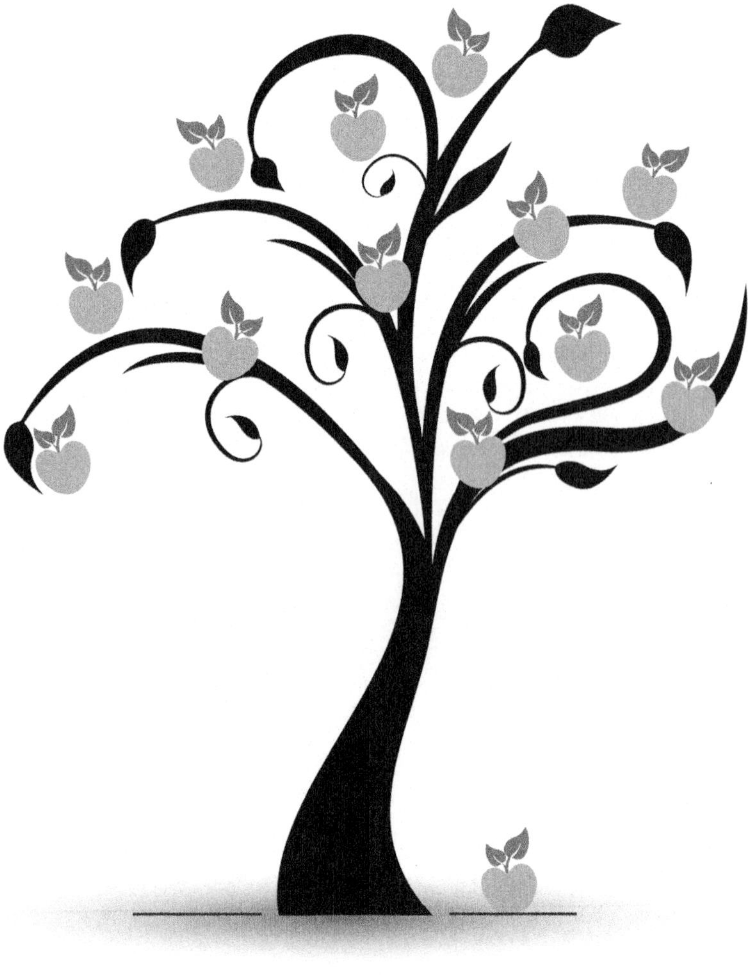

CHAPTER 18

Toxic Relationships

"Love should not make you feel like walking on eggshells."

Emma Xu

There's a reason that whole books are dedicated to the topic of toxic relationships. There's no "one size fits all" to the levels of toxicity. There's no one stereotypical "type" of toxicity. A relationship can have many different combinations of behaviors falling within the commonly known labels of passive, passive-aggressive, and aggressive. The abuse can be mental, emotional, verbal, physical, sexual, or spiritual. There can be many different addictions poisoning the relationship. There can be triggers and trust issues that need to be overcome. This chapter will not be able to cover this kind of information. The main purpose of this book is to discuss mental health, identifying what thoughts are jeopardizing one's mental health, and equipping the reader to overcome these thoughts.

That being said, toxic relationships can uniquely fall into three categories. First, they are often the *result* of an unhealthy thought life. Have you ever noticed that some people seem to move from one toxic relationship to another? That's not to say that this person is the main source of toxicity. Unfortunately, some people seem to be abuse-magnets. I've personally known some of the kindest, most merciful, faithful individuals whose beautiful character was manipulated and used against them. If you notice this pattern, it's important to look at the core beliefs that may be attracting and allowing you to be pulled into one toxic relationship after another.

Secondly, many people feel *trapped* in a toxic relationship because of wrong core beliefs. This person may not necessarily bounce from one toxic relationship to another, but is stuck in the same one year after year, perhaps a lifetime, all because of having wrong core beliefs.

Third, if it wasn't an unhealthy core belief which attracted the toxic relationship or entrapped the person within it, then the relationship will in and of itself *create* poor mental health. Most people can't be exposed to chemical toxins without it affecting their physical health, and the same is true for our mental health. Within this environment, the brain is having to process toxic information on a consistent basis, and the more that toxic information is "ingested" mentally, the stronger the neural pathways which carry that toxic line of thinking will become. Even some of the strongest people I know have developed a negative mental stronghold when placed in a toxic environment for long enough. A once confident, joyful, and optimistic person can come out of a toxic relationship beaten down and reeling from the effects of what felt like a war against their very being.

In short, toxic relationships are a direct assault on who you are and for what purpose you were created. We are created to love and to be loved. We are created for relationship, and those relationships are intended to nourish, protect, and guide us into the exploration of the world around us and our own self-discovery. Ultimately, relationships are intended to be a reflection of the relationship between the Trinity as well as His relationship with us.

Thus, our view of God and of ourselves is intricately intertwined with how we interact with others in a relationship. The healthier our view of God and of ourselves, the better we'll be able to nourish healthy relationships and protect ourselves from toxic ones.

Our relationships with others are meant to compliment, not complete us. Only God can be our "fullness" … fullness of joy, fullness of peace, fullness of strength. He is our Source, and no one else—not even yourself. If we find ourselves trying to fill a hole with another person's attention or affection, we leave ourselves vulnerable to the wrong kind of attention. In our desperation to be with someone, we may allow it to be *anyone*, even someone who will tear us down, control us, or neglect us.

This book has already covered many of these negative thoughts, and has hopefully lifted you up to believe that you are not your thoughts, and you are not your actions—you are the beloved of the Father, the chosen bride of Jesus, the apple of His eye, the delight of Him who created you and sustains you. You were in His heart since before the creation of the world—planned, protected, and cherished. He rescues you from shame and will cover you with His love. You're not alone. You are *loveable*.

It's one thing to intellectually accede to these truths, and it's another thing to truly identify with them. Most Christians can recite verse upon verse about God's love, but they do not live in it. Often, people dance around the fire of His presence with their Bible studies and busy-ness of servanthood, all while avoiding actually stepping into it. Stepping in can be scary; it will reveal every part of you that remains in darkness.

So how can you tell if you are only intellectually acceding to His love versus truly identifying with it and abiding in it? Look at the surrounding fruit to see what tree you're actually in. No self-deprecating thoughts can grow from the Tree of Life, nor can anxiety or hatred or hopelessness.

I want to pull back the mask of some common "toxins" dressed up as God's truth. Scripture is God-breathed and carries His Life and Truth. It reveals His very nature, Love. However, the words themselves, taken out of context (out of His nature) do not carry life. In fact, they can be twisted and used for death. Does that statement feel like a bomb was just dropped?

God's word is Truth, and Satan is the Father of Lies. Satan is described in John 8:44 as "a murderer from the beginning, and does not stand in the truth, because there is no truth in him. When he speaks a lie, he speaks *from his own resources*, for he is a liar and the father of it." So if Satan can't speak the truth, then how can he quote God's word? (... crickets chirping ...) After all, Satan used none other than the Word of God to tempt Jesus, saying, "If

You are the Son of God, throw Yourself down. For it is written: 'He shall give His angels charge over you,' and, 'In their hands they shall bear you up, lest you dash your foot against a stone'" (Matthew 4:6).

Satan may have been speaking the words of truth, but he was speaking them from his own resources, such that the words carried only deception and death. In essence, he was twisting Scripture to tempt Jesus to jump to his death, and if He didn't, then He must not be—or have enough faith that He is—God's Son. Think about this: God's words, intended for loving comfort of His protection, were somehow twisted to encourage self-destructive behavior!

Scripture is too often used outside of the resources of God's love and instead used within Satan's resources to control, manipulate, and place a darkness over our hearts, hiding God's true nature. Scripture has been used to justify slavery. It has been used to demean women. It has been used to foster xenophobia. Satan is, unfortunately, masterful at manipulating Scripture, and was able to shield even the experts in it from recognizing the Author of it: "You search the Scriptures, for in them you think you have eternal life; and these are they which testify of Me. But you are not willing to come to Me that you may have life" (John 5:39-40).

I've seen pastors use Scripture to subdue their congregations under themselves rather than raise them up in Christ. Finally, I've seen Scripture used to keep men and women in toxic relationships. The thing about manipulation is that it is most effective when it plays upon what's most important to a person and when it uses some form of "truth"—a perverted truth.

I realize that not everyone reading this may be a Christian. However, I think that pointing out what can be specifically twisted and targeted at Christians can also be understood and applied to general core beliefs that are damaging, regardless of your religion. Here are some of the beliefs that are keeping many Christians in bondage to a toxic relationship:

- Love covers a multitude of sins, so I must not be loving if I hold my partner accountable.

- God says to forgive, so, again, I can't hold this against my partner. I need to forgive and forget, even if things never change.

- Love is patient. I realize that we've been in the same pattern year after year, but I need to remain patient until things change.

- God says that my body isn't my own, so I should let my partner decide what I do, or use my body as he/she wants. I belong to him/her, not myself.

- The Bible says to submit to one another, so it doesn't matter what I think or feel, I just need to submit.

- I need to prefer others over myself. It doesn't matter what my partner is doing to me, I should be selfless and loving enough to take it.

- Love is slow to anger. If I feel angry about how I'm being treated, that must mean I'm unloving. If I'm angry about my situation, it's just a sign that I need to grow spiritually.

- Christ died for us while we were still sinners, so if I want to be like Him, then I must be able to take whatever mistreatment towards me. If I can't handle abuse, then I must not have died to myself, yet.

- The Bible says I can't waver on what I'm praying about, so if I'm praying for my partner, then I need to believe this situation will change. I better stay the course.

- I can't please God without faith, so I have to believe this situation will get better. If I give up, it will be like I gave up faith, and that would displease God. I don't want to disappoint Him.

- Jesus promised us that we'd be persecuted. I should rejoice that I can suffer this attack on me. I need to be willing to endure anything.

- I know that my partner calls me all sorts of names, but I should be strong enough to know who I am in Christ. If I were a mature Christian, this wouldn't even affect me.

The list can go on and on. Notice, there is always an element of truth. However, these truths are the mask. What is really being used are the resources of the "father of lies", meant to steal, kill, and destroy. Each of these beliefs not only misuse elements of God's words to keep someone in an abusive situation, they also carry shame if the person were to ever stand up for him or herself, or to leave the situation. It's a double-entrapment.

Of course, there are many beautiful testimonies of relationships being healed, even within the most severely toxic ones. It may be through focused re-training of the mind to facilitate healthy attitudes and behaviors. Sometimes, those within it suddenly "see the Light" and have a miraculous turnaround. God's grace is working within each situation. He is always there for every person, with the light on in the kitchen, wanting them to see and sit down with Him. We can pray for that. However, you are not less "spiritual" if you recognize a repetitive cycle in someone's behavior and decide that it's time for you to leave them to their own decisions. *You are not their personal savior.* Even in the presence of the real Savior, many did not have a change of heart. Jesus recognized this, and He didn't blame Himself for not being able to get through to the Pharisees, for instance.

Whatever part you play within the toxic relationship, don't allow condemnation to settle over you. Shame and condemnation undermine any positive change of thoughts and behavior, because these are contrary to the Tree of Life. Satan has been called the "accuser of the brethren" (Revelation 12:10). How does he manage to accuse? Again, he's a masterful manipulator of God's word. He knows God's law by heart, though it is not in his heart. And he'll use it to sentence you to death.

I know a woman who had been in an abusive marriage for many years. She was consistently beaten and raped. She was thrown down the stairs. She had 22 of her teeth knocked out. Despite all the physical abuse, she told me that the emotional abuse always hurts more. Your body can be hurt, yes, but being told in so many different ways that you're worthless can cause damage to the soul that is much harder to heal. She was controlled, manipulated, and living in fear.

Several times throughout this relationship, she reached out to her church leaders. Can you guess what they said? Let's just say, they didn't represent a God who defends the weak or upholds the cause of the oppressed. They didn't represent a God who saves the afflicted or binds up the brokenhearted. They revealed a God who freely extended mercy to the abuser, yet none to the victim. He supposedly didn't care to set the captive free that day. Instead, she was sent home to be the better Christian.

Tragically, this is not uncommon. Some people have been sent to their death in a toxic relationship by some perverted view of God's expectation. Those who are not physically in danger of death, still feel themselves dying inside.

I should note here that, obviously, relationships take work, and I'm not encouraging anyone to bail out at the first sign of any problem. Also, one must be honest about their own attitudes and behaviors that may be contributing to the toxicity. Be humble. Take responsibility for the part you play in the relationship. On the other hand, enduring toxic relationships is not a Christian rite of passage, serving as a means of making you a stronger Christian. In the end, allowing these abusive relationships to continue undermines the Source of your strength. You won't be able to see God correctly. Instead, while you're gasping for air, all you feel is Him holding your head under water.

To truly "die to yourself" in biblical terms is not a denial of your inherent value, nor a hatred for your emotions or desire to be loved. In fact, you can't die to yourself unless you know your value and you embrace that you're created to be loved. Dying to yourself is simply resting in the arms of your Father, knowing that He'll take care of you—you don't have the power to make Him love you, He already does.

It's impossible to fully love Him when you don't know His love. Remember, "We love Him because He first loved us" (1 John 4:19). Remove the mask that portrays God as your heavenly Abuser. It can be hard to admit this wrong belief, but sadly, it is the case for many that feel trapped in toxic relationships.

WHAT TO DO IN A POSSIBLY TOXIC RELATIONSHIP

Everyone will get involved in an unhealthy relationship at some point in their life. It may be an alcoholic parent, a verbally abusive spouse, or a child who continually lies to and steals from you. It would be irresponsible of me to give blanket advice for what to do when you find yourself in a toxic relationship. Every situation is different and thus the approaches toward healing the relationship will differ. The decision of if or when to leave the relationship also shouldn't be generalized. What I can say to everyone, however, is that boundaries are a healthy and necessary part of relationships. Don't feel guilty about setting boundaries in your life. Also, if you are at any point in fear over your safety, please do not hesitate to separate yourself and find help.

At some time in your life, you will come to a crossroad. If you're unsure how to proceed, please consider the following options:

1. Keep a journal. In many relationships there's a partner that can make you question your sanity. I often hear cases of a spouse telling their partner that they are overreacting. They come to me wondering, "Am I crazy?" If you can't trust your feelings, write the situation and the corresponding emotions down. Do that for a couple of weeks. This way you'll be better able to assess the situation. When we are in a situation and emotions are running high, it's easy to read it the wrong way. By journaling, you can reflect on it later.

2. If you're questioning whether your situation is toxic, seek outside counsel, whether it be seeking out professional help or seeking out the many published resources available on the topic.

3. Practice placing your thoughts on trial, as previously discussed in this book. Do you feel like you should accept abusive treatments? If so, why? What are your core beliefs that lead you to that conclusion? Is that belief rational? Is it healthy? Is that belief founded in the resources of God's love? Do you have any fears? What are they and why do you have that fear? What skills and resources can you draw upon to help you through that fear?

    Another thing I suggest is asking yourself, especially if you're a parent: If my children (who I love and want to protect) were to find themselves in this situation, what would I want for them? Place yourself as an outside observer. Oftentimes, a person is in a toxic relationship because they don't have the proper love for themselves. Therefore, try to imagine someone you love in the situation. What would your advice to them be?

4. If you do decide to leave, always remember why you are doing it. Here's a tricky trap into which many people can fall: you are told to not make any decisions based on emotions or "impulsivity". On the other hand, the toxic relationship is continually painful. At some point, you'll feel angry about how you're being treated. It's important to remember that although you shouldn't impulsively make any decision in the heat of the moment, that doesn't mean that anger is the enemy. God created you with emotions. Scripture depicts God as feeling the emotion of anger at times. It shouldn't be our source of direction, but it can be a built-in warning system letting us know that something isn't as God intended it. God *feels* for those who are oppressed. Feelings are not the enemy. Don't allow them to control you, but don't ignore them, either.

   Remember your reasons for leaving and that will help you stay the course of your original decision.

5. If you decide to leave, realize that running away isn't the ultimate answer. While separating yourself can be necessary for healing, it does not automatically fix all the negative core beliefs that either led you into that relationship in the first place, or have been formed because of it. Be intentional about your mental and emotional healing. Don't allow the toxic relationship to affect the rest of your life, even after you're no longer physically in it.

6. Give yourself grace and time to adjust. Be aware that you will be going through all the different emotions. At times you will be sad, other times angry, other times elated to feel free, and then somehow tempted to go back at times. Acknowledge how you feel, and give yourself the time to process through it. God is walking with you wherever you are in the process of healing.

7. Allow yourself to mourn the relationship. In nearly every abusive relationship, there were moments that felt like love and happiness—the "good times"—and these will naturally be missed. You're allowed to feel loss. Resist any thoughts that are shameful or condemning in any way. Always keep in mind why you decided your course of action and process everything from the foundation of knowing you deserve to be loved.

8. Forgive. Forgiving does not mean that you continue to allow the behavior. It doesn't mean that you magically forget all that hurt you. It also doesn't mean that you continue in the relationship. What forgiveness does is cuts the toxic strings between you and that person, entrusting God to be the judge. If you hold onto the strings of unforgiveness, you'll be puppeted around by them. That's not freedom.

    Forgiveness also recognizes that it's not about making the other person the enemy. There is no "I'm good and they were bad". Remember, we all fall short. The good we have in us is God shining through us, and God's light can shine through every person, no matter how abusive their behavior can be at times. You can recognize that light in the person while maintaining perspective of the situation as a whole.

9. Enforce necessary boundaries. Decide which behavior is unacceptable and communicate the boundaries necessary to prevent that behavior from happening. This is true whether you've decided to remain in the relationship or have left it. Without proper boundaries, there is no barrier to stop toxic behavior. Without boundaries, it can be difficult to feel safe enough to focus on healing. Remember, you are worth being protected.

Question:

1. What is a healthy boundary you can place in your relationship(s) and how can you enforce it?

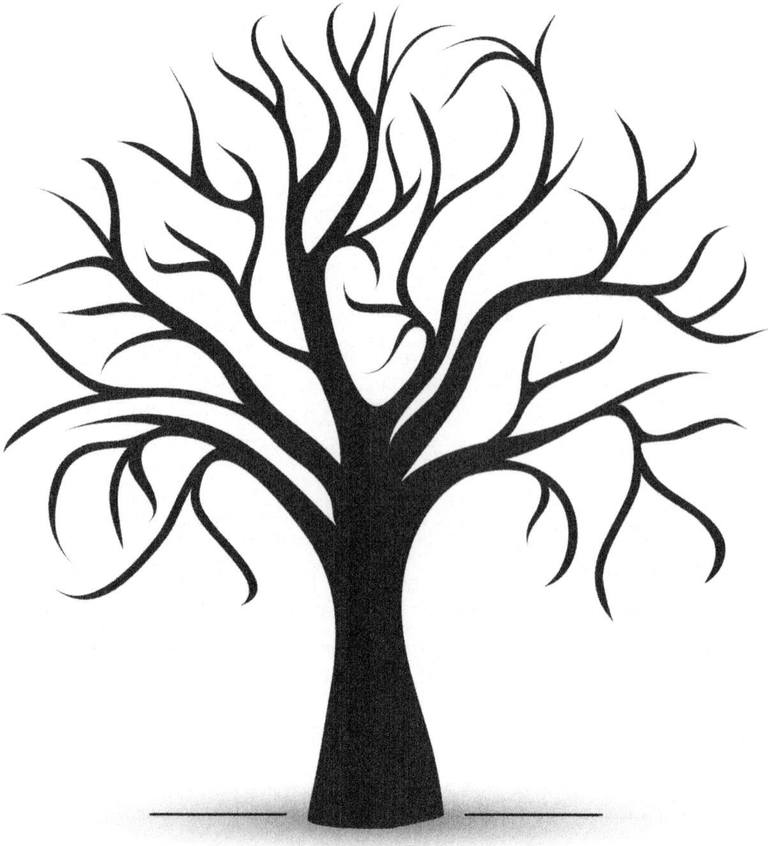

CHAPTER 19

Self-Destructive Behavior

"All forms of self-defeating behavior are unseen and unconscious, which is why their existence is denied."

Vernon Howard

Self-destructive behavior many times begins in adolescence, that wonderful age when you're growing up, but lack the skills to overcome stress or anxiety. Because we have few skills to calm these emotions, we frantically search for something to help us feel better. Drinking, binge eating, and becoming sexually active outside of a committed relationship are all examples of self-destructive behavior. Once again we stand before this big hole inside of all of us and we self-medicate. Many times these behaviors are our go-to because they numb the pain, even if only for a second.

Unfortunately we have not been taught a healthy way of coping, and thus it becomes the ingrained method of managing anxiety and self-esteem by the time you reach adulthood. These behaviors are very hard to let go of; they are addictive in nature.

As we look down into this hole of pain inside of us, we see Him holding us in our pain, finding us when we have lost ourselves. When we come to Jesus, we discover that He loves us completely, including our "hidden side". His love comes to us without any conditions. That is the way He asks us to love each other, whole and without any conditions.

We are free to do whatever we want, but take note that sin has its own punishment. "Accepted Sin" is very brutal to us, and blinds us to Him. Yet, we continue to do the most foolish thing we can do, and then we hit REPEAT. It ends up trapping us and making us sick.

There is a way out of this cycle of self-destructive behavior.

- There is nothing shameful in asking for help.

- Don't believe the negative self-talk, the streams of conversation that are unhelpful to your mind. Challenge those thoughts that go against the knowledge of God.

- If you want to quit and you make a mistake, don't see it as a failure. See it as a lesson learned. If you see a little fire in your kitchen, will you just leave it to burn the house down? No! You extinguish it, and you learn not to leave the stove top unmanned.

- Become aware of the triggers that set off before self-destructive behavior starts.

- Breathe deeply. Know that He is in you; He's got you. You are gonna be okay.

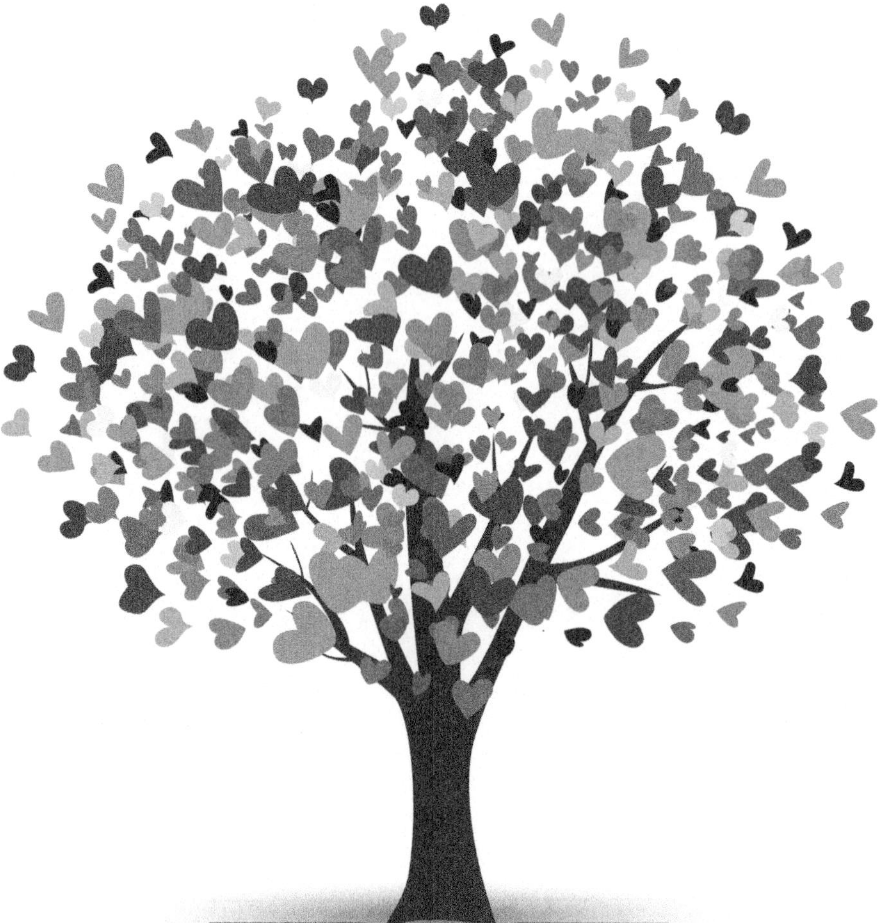

CHAPTER 20

Self-Care

"When you recover or discover something that nourishes your soul and brings joy, care enough about yourself to make room for it in your life."

Jean Shinoda Bolen

Ever felt like running away? Who is willing to join me? Just take a break from Life as we know it and sit and do....nothing. Absolutely nothing.

I would be running around the whole day, between work sessions, errands, horses, children, dogs, cooking, laundry, etc., etc., and many times it would feel like my inside was spinning. I would be standing still, but I would still be running.

Depending on the cultural influences around you, mentioning "self-care" may elicit different and sometimes negative feelings. In the women-can-do-everything and super-mom culture, self-care can feel like a weakness. After all, strong women can just keep on going, right? It's not just women; men also feel the pressure on their shoulders to keep pressing through the mess and stress.

Another culture that can undermine self-care is the Christian church culture. Surprised? With all the messages preached on selflessness and self-sacrifice and preferring others over ourselves, and always being the faithful servant whenever there's a need ... (deep breath) ... the originally beautiful biblical intention of these messages can be misconstrued to mean that we shouldn't feel the need to take care of our souls and bodies. The need to take a break and nurture yourself can feel like spiritual inadequacy ... and there comes that condemnation again!

Here's a verse that is speaking about loving another person, particularly one's spouse. However, there's a key point within this verse that forms the foundation for being able to offer that love to others. Ephesians 5:28-29 tells husbands to "love their wives as their own bodies. He who loves his wife loves himself. After all, no one ever hated their own body, but they feed and care for their body, just as Christ does the church." Do you notice how it's not only assumed, it's essential for the husband to love, nourish, and cherish his own body in order for him to properly do the same for his wife? Wow! Care for your own body!

Need more permission to care for yourself? Matthew 22:39 tells us to "love your neighbor" ... that's the common highlighted aspect of this verse, but it's equally important to note that it specifies "love your neighbor as yourself". *As yourself.* How well do you love yourself? It's impossible to truly love others and serve them if you don't know how to love and nurture yourself.

Never before has self-care been so important. I've seen the effect of a pandemic, loss of livelihood, hopelessness, and stress—in a society gripped in fear due to an unseen enemy. Self-care may sound like a cliché, but you'll thank me later. Working these activities into your routine is sure to impact your day-to-day life positively.

PRACTICE MINDFULNESS

Studies have shown the benefits of mindfulness, the way it impacts your brain, and how good it is for your wellbeing. If you're still wondering what mindfulness is and get confused between mindfulness and meditation, mindfulness is a quality; it's a way of life. It's shutting down the autopilot and tuning in to awareness. You will start looking at things differently, appreciate life more and realize you should not be entitled to anything. Know that today is a gift, you will never have today again.

Have you looked at the trees? Have you seen how beautiful the flowers grow in Spring? Who calls the sun to shine on it? Who sent His Son to shine on us? The same God upholding Creation is upholding and maintaining every single living organism on earth. When you understand that, you'll understand how small we really are.

Life is a gift; don't ever take it for granted.

SPEND SOME TIME ALONE

If you are spending all day taking care of others, you need some time for yourself to do the things you enjoy. Go for a massage, read a book, and be a bit protective of your time.

I have a time at night that is "Mommy's Time". No one is allowed to ask me for anything, and from 7:30 p.m. to 8:00 p.m. the kitchen is closed. I have coffee and I plan my day. I then make sure most of my early morning chores for the next day are taken care of. I pack school lunches, make sure their clothes are ready and ironed, decide what I will wear the next day and get it ready. Basic ideas like getting things ready ahead of time can help you ease your mind, avoid the stress of "rush" ... and give you five minutes more to snooze the next morning.

GO EXERCISE IN NATURE

The benefits of exercise are astounding. Exercise can reduce insomnia, stimulate brain growth, and even act as an antidepressant. It's amazing what those feel-good hormones do to your wellbeing, and they get released when we exercise!

LEARN A NEW SKILL

Spending time to learn a new skill such as surfing, cooking, or playing an instrument can help make your life more interesting. Be sure to pick a skill that is important to you, something you can enjoy when you see the end product.

CONTEMPLATIVE PRAYER

I remember as a little girl, I would read the children's bible with all the beautiful illustrations, and I found it comforting to read the gospels. I would read about the multiplication of food, the sick being healed, and the dead being raised. When I was nine, I got my very first Bible and I started reading it.

One day, the Bible fell open to Isaiah 43. As I read it, it felt as though hot oil was dripping over my head and my hands. I could not explain this to anyone, I did not have the vocabulary to express what happened. Decades later, I look back at that day and remember the smell of baked bread and the sound of laughter. I can see myself sitting on my bed and being in complete awe. Since that day, whenever I am scared or apprehensive about the future and what it may hold, I begin thinking about Isaiah 43 and what that means to me.

> "But now, thus says the Lord, who created you, O Jacob, and He who formed you, O Israel: 'Fear not, for I have redeemed you; I have called you by your name; you are Mine. When you pass through the waters, I will be with you; and through the rivers, they shall not overflow you. When you walk through the fire, you shall not be burned, nor shall the flame scorch you. For I am the Lord your God, the Holy One of Israel, your Savior . . .
>
> Since you were precious in My sight, you have been honored, and I have loved you; therefore I will give men for you, and people for your life. Fear not, for I am with you; I will bring your descendants from the east, and gather you from the west; I will say to the north, 'Give them up!' And to the south, 'Do not keep them back!'

Bring My sons from afar, and My daughters from the ends of the earth - everyone who is called by My name, whom I have created for My glory; I have formed him, yes, I have made him.' Bring out the blind people who have eyes, and the deaf who have ears. Let all the nations be gathered together, and let the people be assembled. Who among them can declare this, and show us former things? Let them bring out their witnesses, that they may be justified; or let them hear and say, 'It is truth.'

'You are My witnesses,' says the Lord, 'And My servant whom I have chosen, that you may know and believe Me, and understand that I am He. Before Me there was no God formed, nor shall there be after Me. I, even I, am the Lord, and besides Me there is no savior. I have declared and saved, I have proclaimed, and there was no foreign god among you; therefore you are My witnesses,' says the Lord, 'that I am God. Indeed before the day was, I am He; and there is no one who can deliver out of My hand; I work, and who will reverse it?'"

(Isaiah 43:1-13).

Bliss.

Here's a simple exercise for you:

1. Choose a scripture. Begin with your memory passage for the week.

2. Sit comfortably (but not *too* comfortably), back straight, chest open so the breath is free and open.

3. Read the passage slowly. Savor each phrase. What word, phrase or idea speaks to you?

4. Read the passage again. Where does this passage touch your life? What do you see, hear, touch, or remember?

5. Read the passage a third time. Listen quietly.

6. Note insights, reflections, and personal response to the reading in your journal.

7. Follow the steps in order or go back and forth between them as you feel moved.
8. Finish by waiting for a few moments in silence.

> "... and the peace of God, which surpasses all understanding, will guard your hearts and minds through Christ Jesus. Finally, brethren, whatever things are true, whatever things are noble, whatever things are just, whatever things are pure, whatever things are lovely, whatever things are of good report, if there is any virtue and if there is anything praiseworthy—meditate on these things. The things which you learned and received and heard and saw in me, these do, and the God of peace will be with you" (Philippians 4:7-9).

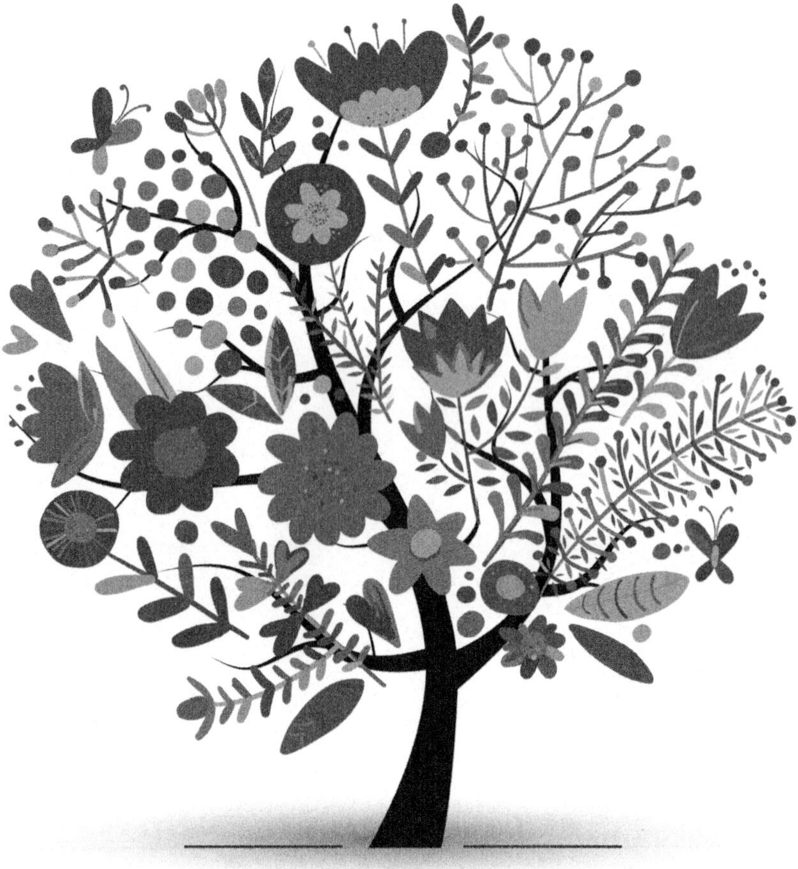

CHAPTER 21

Happiness

"Folks are usually about as happy as they make their minds up to be."

Abraham Lincoln

Are you happy? What makes you happy? Getting that promotion you've been working towards, or how about winning the lotto? Sure, it'll make you happy, but for how long? Sustained happiness takes work, a radical mind shift, restructuring the way you look at life. Happiness is not something you get from the outside, it's something on the inside. If you lost your joy in life and you need to get it back, I encourage you to look at the next exercises. It never fails, and I have seen how this works with 99% of my clients.

BE GRATEFUL.

Be mindful of being grateful. Let's go back to that sandwich we spoke about earlier in the book. Who made the sun shine on the tomato? Who brought the rain? It's absolutely nothing we did. He gives us the sunshine and we participate in whatever He gives us.

Write down three things you are grateful for every day. They may be as small as having coffee with friends or going for a walk. It does not need to be big, you just need to become aware of everything you have in life. Tell your partner or children that you are grateful for them and whatever (small) things they do for you.

Chances are, through this positive reinforcement, they'll also do more to help and they will start being grateful for what they have.

Again, we need to learn how to self-regulate. When we are able to do that, we can help others to do so, also. Prisons are full, because people do not know how to self-regulate. You are *not* your thoughts. Your thoughts may tell you to hurt someone, but they are merely thoughts. You give power to them by meditating on them and then acting upon them. If you reject the toxic thought, it has no power over you.

BE KIND.

I challenge you to do something for someone else today for no reason at all. You'll be surprised at what it does for your brain. Make a conscious effort to make someone smile. Pay for a stranger's coffee at the cafe. Help carry bags for an elderly person. Tell a cleaner that they are really good at their job.

People who've seen me regularly would many times leave a voice message on my phone to thank me for the help, etc. Many would say, "I love you for what you've done for me. Thank you!" One day, I asked my dad what he thought about this. He recognized that their reactions were because there is so little hope left in the world for people. He then told me to "go be the hope for others."

I really loved that idea; I want to be the hope for others. I encourage you to be the hope for others, too. Ultimately, we all have hope. *He* is our hope and our Light. It doesn't matter how dark the situation appears to be, look to Him. He is Hope.

Have grace for yourself! Have forgiveness for yourself! Be kind to yourself!

EXERCISE.

The positive effects of exercise are astounding. Physically active people have increased energy, superior immune systems, and a frequent sense of accomplishment. Exercise can reduce insomnia, stimulate brain growth, and even act as an antidepressant. It's amazing what those feel-good hormones do to your being, and they get released when we exercise.

You don't need to start running marathons tomorrow or become a gym junkie. Simply start by taking the stairs as you go to work instead of the elevator. Take fifteen-minute walks during lunch or take a bike ride and enjoy the scenery. Look at everything He has made in childlike wonder.

FOSTER RELATIONSHIPS WITH YOUR LOVED ONES.

Those who are dedicated to spending time with friends and family show the highest levels of happiness. Spend time with your loved ones; you never know what tomorrow will bring. My grandma used to say: Bring me flowers while I am still here, don't bring them to my funeral. If time is a problem, make time. Schedule time to catch up.

BREATHE.

The first thing we do when we enter this world is breathe. Breath is the only thing that will stay with us our whole life; it never leaves us. Nothing is permanent. Friends will come and go. You might move between continents, yet breath travels with you. When you get angry, your breath changes. When you get sad, your breath changes. And before we return to dust, we blow out our last breath.

We thought it was oxygen, but it is you, Lord. You are the breath we breathe. You are Breath.

Question:

1. What makes you happy?

2. How can you organize your life to do more of it?

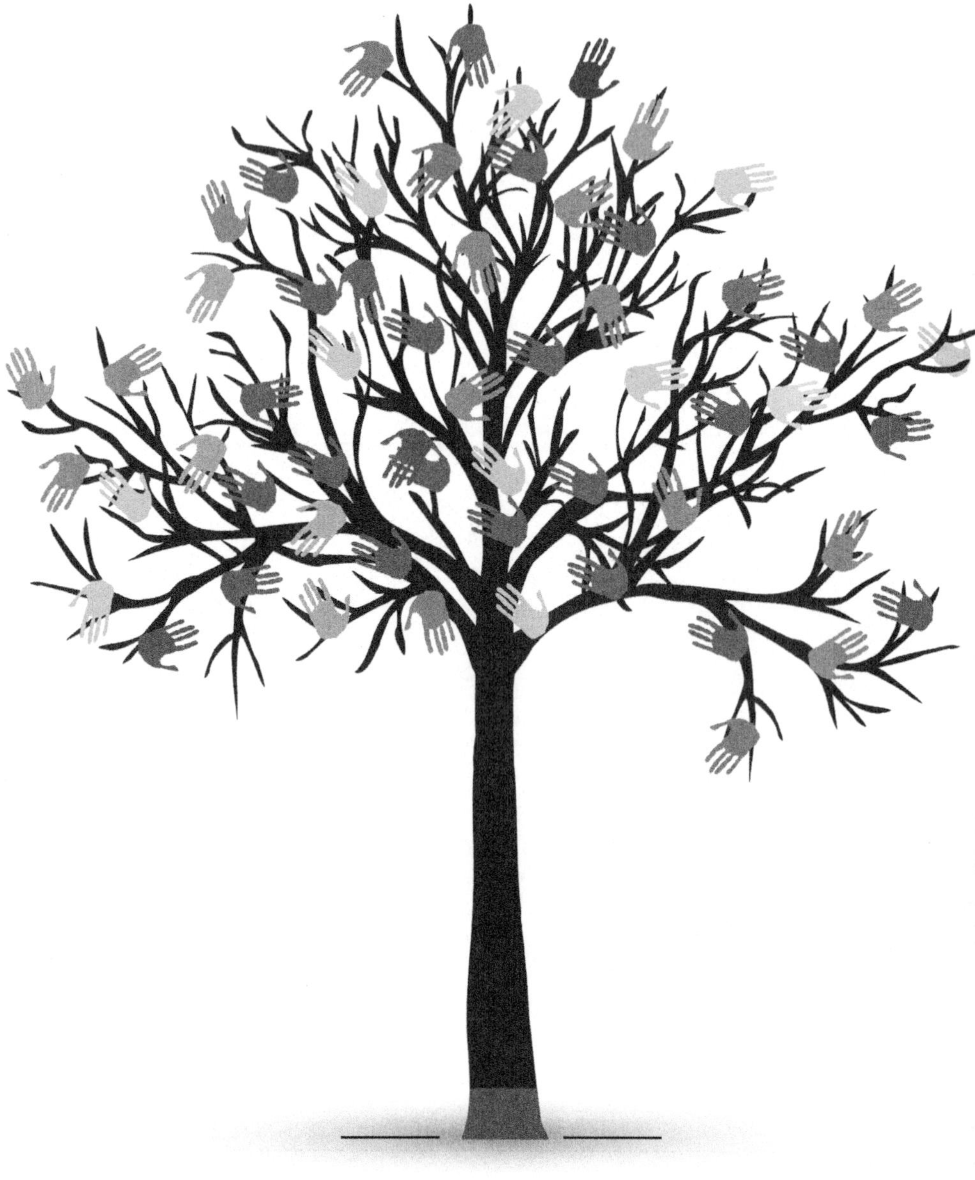

CHAPTER 22

Quantum Entanglement

"Spooky action at a distance."

Albert Einstein

We are all connected ...

John 1 describes that the Light was shining in the darkness (in all of humanity), but the darkness could not see it. It did not stop the Light from shining though; it kept on shining through all of creation, all the galaxies, and the whole universe.

The Light of God is magnified in a Person, Jesus Christ. The Light is God's DNA and was given to us. Now, we are the light shining in the world. His very DNA is shining in us.

If this Light shines through all of humanity, it means we are all connected. It sounds a bit new age, I realize, but they may not be as far off as you think. (I feel like hugging a tree.) The same Life source is flowing through us; we are all family ... we are entangled, and what we do has a ripple effect on the rest of creation. Once we grasp this entanglement, we will start taking care of the earth and of each other. Everything is connected.

Looking at it from this angle, we look at the words of Jesus, who tells us to forgive each other and to love our enemies. It has little to do with a victim mentality, but rather it has to do with our wiring. If we are wired to love and forgive, and yet we don't, we go against our design. We should love our enemies, because He is also in our enemies, upholding them. If we hate our enemies, who is it we are hating? Ask yourself this.

Entanglement is a primary law of quantum physics, it demonstrates how connected everything is. Let's look at forgiveness. If we are indeed entangled and I don't have forgiveness towards you, I will stay entangled in a situation that is painful to me. Everything you say and do will hurt, and it would be as if you are hurting me every time I think about you. By forgiving you, I am disentangling myself from the situation and I can go on. You are no longer affected by it; it's not toxic anymore.

HOW PRESENT ARE YOU?

How easy is it to live in the past? To think about the things we could have done, would have done? The fight we had with a partner, the argument with a sibling years ago … If you can't seem to shake things off and you find it hard to get closure, have you asked yourself why you are holding on to this memory? Isn't it time to let go?

Maybe you don't even know what is holding you back, but you keep walking around with the world on your shoulders. As this book is about awareness, I want you to take a few minutes and look at the following questions.

1. What is the very first memory you can remember? Is it a good or bad memory? Tell me about it.

2. Who is with you in the memory?

3. What is the impression you have of yourself in this memory? What are the impressions you have of those with you?

4. How much has this memory impacted your decision making, thoughts, and behavior?

5. Do you believe God was with you during this time? Why?

6. Has this experience changed your view of God? Has it changed your view of others, or of yourself? Tell me about it.

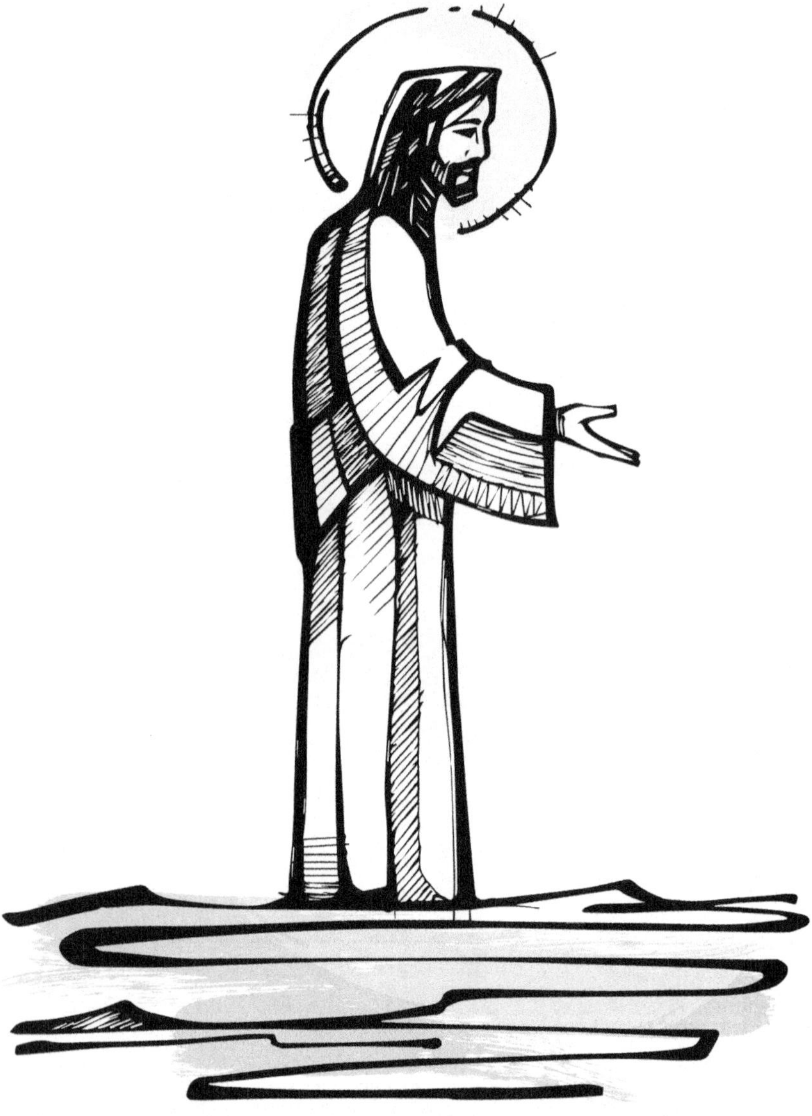

CHAPTER 23
Build Resilience

"For a righteous man may fall seven times and rise again."

(Proverbs 24:16)

I think I was around fourteen years old when I read this poem by *Rudyard Kipling*, and I am sure this is where my love for studying human behavior started.

If

If you can keep your head when all about you
    Are losing theirs and blaming it on you,
If you can trust yourself when all men doubt you,
    But make allowance for their doubting too;
If you can wait and not be tired by waiting,
    Or being lied about, don't deal in lies,
Or being hated, don't give way to hating,
    And yet don't look too good, nor talk too wise:

If you can dream—and not make dreams your master;
    If you can think—and not make thoughts your aim;
If you can meet with Triumph and Disaster
    And treat those two impostors just the same;
If you can bear to hear the truth you've spoken
    Twisted by knaves to make a trap for fools,

Or watch the things you gave your life to, broken,
    And stoop and build 'em up with worn-out tools:

If you can make one heap of all your winnings
    And risk it on one turn of pitch-and-toss,
And lose, and start again at your beginnings
    And never breathe a word about your loss;
If you can force your heart and nerve and sinew
    To serve your turn long after they are gone,
And so hold on when there is nothing in you
    Except the Will which says to them: 'Hold on!'

If you can talk with crowds and keep your virtue,
    Or walk with Kings—nor lose the common touch,
If neither foes nor loving friends can hurt you,
    If all men count with you, but none too much;
If you can fill the unforgiving minute
    With sixty seconds' worth of distance run,
Yours is the Earth and everything that's in it,
    And—which is more—you'll be a Man, my son!

Be resilient, don't let anything get you down—that is probably the one thing I am obsessed with teaching my children. You need to be resilient in life. When life knocks you down, you get back up again. You need to take responsibility for your happiness in life and create lemonade from those lemons.

Building resiliency is one of the cornerstones of cognitive behavioral therapy (CBT). Resilience is the ability to persevere, to adapt, and to bounce back from difficult situations. Resilience helps us find contentment and enjoyment in life. In short, resilience greatly contributes to good mental and emotional health, and helps us to survive, cope, and feel in control, even during turbulent times. Emotional resilience helps to calm your frantic mind after encountering a difficult situation. Just like emotional intelligence and social intelligence, our resilience will develop for the rest of our lives.

Resilience is the ability to cope with whatever life throws at you, and bounce back stronger and more steadfast than before. As Nelson Mandela stated, "The greatest glory in living lies not in never falling, but in rising every time we fall."

THE 4 S'S TO BUILDING RESILIENCE

Recall a recent example of resilience, What did you do to overcome the situation? Briefly describe this event.

Now I want you to look at the situation you are facing. It may be losing your job, or an ended relationship. How will you bounce back?

Let's look at what is called the "4 S's" game plan:

Support: Identify people who support you. Who are those people who are always on your side? Who can you call at 2:00 in the morning when you need to go to the hospital? Who will stand by you? Write down their names below.

Strategies: Throughout this book I gave you a lot of strategies on how to cope with negative thoughts and feelings. Will you start journaling your thoughts? Will you identify the negative automatic thoughts? Did you start exercising? Did you confide in a friend? What did you do previously to overcome a challenge, and can it be applied here?

Sagacity: Sagacity is that powerful wisdom onto which you hold. He will never leave me nor forsake me! I am the righteousness in Christ! If you are not Christian and would rather use another means, you can look at poems, a song, a novel, or whatever speaks to your spirit. It can even be an inspiring word from a friend or family member. Write down your sagacity below.

Solution-Focused Behavior: CBT is focused on solution and is goal orientated. Unlike traditional psychology, it's a high-impact form of psychotherapy. What solution-seeking behaviors did you display to help you actively deal with the problem? Did you seek out new information, or plan ahead, or negotiate, or speak up and voice your opinion, or ask others for help? Write down the solution-seeking behavior that will help you in this situation.

_____

_____

_____

_____

_____

Let's use an example:

You are heartbroken over a relationship that ended.

1) Support

- Call my mom.
- Make an appointment with my therapist.
- Make a lunch date with my best friend.

2) Strategies

- Start journaling.
- Restructure my thoughts.
- Write down everything for which I am grateful.
- Practice mindfulness.
- Go for a walk in the park.
- Spring clean my home.
- Meditate on the good things in life (Philippians 4:8).
- Put my thoughts on trial.

3) Sagacity

- The joy of the Lord is my strength (Nehemiah 8:10).
- Learn from your mistakes.
- Meditate on His unending goodness
- This too shall pass.
- When one door closes, a better one opens.

4) Solution Seeking

Think about how you can better yourself and find peace in YOU.

- Journal
- Don't allow your mind to meditate on the negative for too long, switch back to the positive side. You are beautifully made, unique and loveable. Their loss!
- Know your worth and own it.
- Bounce back; you are stronger than you think.
- Be resilient.

My dad would always tell me, "Baby, when the hills seem hard for you to walk, remember to keep on going, because the downhills are coming and you can run down."

God gave me more insight on this. When your feet are hurting and you can't walk anymore, I need you to keep your eyes on the mountaintop. He is the God of the mountain, and the God of the valley. As you walk through the valley, He will walk beside you, and as you walk to the mountain, He is with you. He knows what awaits you on the mountaintop, and His plans are to prosper you.

Keep on walking

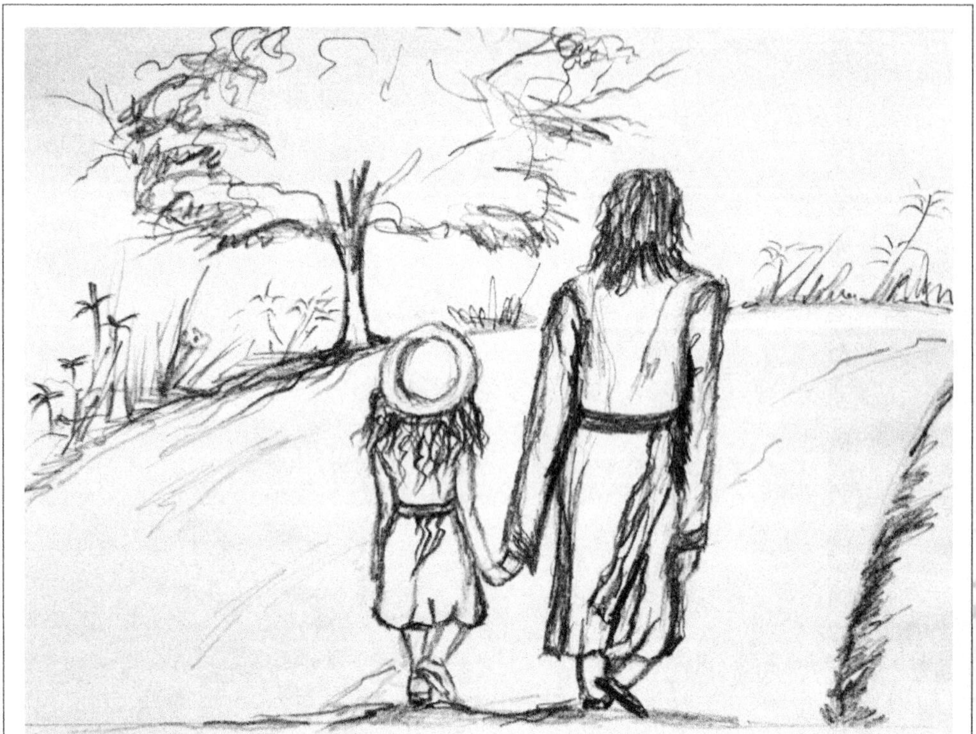

CHAPTER 24

He Swallowed Death in Victory

"Only a moment you stayed, but what an imprint your footprints have left on our hearts."

Dorothy Ferguson, Little Footprints

How hard is it to say goodbye? It breaks our hearts. *If we could just have one more day ... just one more*, we think. We would change things; we would spend more time with them. We would hug them and never let go. We would tell them how loved they are and what an impact they made in our life. If we just had more time, more time to say we are sorry. More time to forgive, let live, and let go. We would hold their hand, hold them close to us, breathe them in, and never let go.

As a child, I really suffered with this thought. The thought that I would not see my loved ones if they should die, or if I should die. I did not understand all the eschatology, and the thought that I would be without my family and God ... it petrified me.

Thinking about it now, I think things started turning around for me on the 14th of July, 1995, when I met the Man in the White Robe. My mom would often remind me how I looked at life when I woke up from the coma. Flowers are not just flowers to me, not anymore. I see life inside of the flowers. I see His Light inside of everyone. I remember the fragrance of Life, and now know what it means—He swallowed death in victory.

Maybe that is why the early Christians had no fear of death. They were thrown into the colosseum with wild animals as a sport, but they knew that there was no place He was not. There is no place He does not dwell.

> "Where can I go from Your Spirit?
> Or where can I flee from Your presence?
> If I ascend into heaven, You are there;
> If I make my bed in hell, behold, You are there.
> If I take the wings of the morning,
> And dwell in the uttermost parts of the sea,
> Even there Your hand shall lead me,
> And Your right hand shall hold me.
> If I say, 'Surely the darkness shall fall on me,'
> Even the night shall be light about me;
> Indeed, the darkness shall not hide from You,
> But the night shines as the day;
> The darkness and the light are both alike to You."
> (Psalm 139:7)

I don't think they were ever taught a gospel of separation. They would die for what they knew was the truth; they had no fear of death. While they lived it was, "It is no longer I who live, but Christ lives in me: (Galatians 2:20). And when they faced death, it was, "For to me, to live is Christ, and to die is gain" (Philippians 1:21).

Ultimately, it is the goodness of God that leads us to repentance, not the fear of hell fire. That is what Paul preached. Yet, today we tend to focus on the latter. When we discuss repentance, do you think it should be turning in terror from the flames of hell? Or do you think it should be turning to see the open arms of a loving Father? Which one of these most captures your heart?

There is no place in the universe you can go where He is not; He is everywhere. Even if you go to the outermost parts of the universe, He is there. I believe we all come from God, and when we die, we return to Him. We were made from dust and we will return to dust, meeting our Source face-to-face. The consuming Fire who burns with a passion for humanity and wants no one to be lost ... He took away the sting of death.

No one is ever forgotten. In the words of Mary Poppins, *"Nothing is gone forever, only out of place"*.[1] She would remind the kids of this very truth when they lost something dear to them. This stuck with me: Nothing is ever gone; it's simply not in the place we would normally look for it. It's the same with our loved ones; they are not gone.

> You were never forgotten.
> You were never forsaken.
> You were never left behind.
>
> You were lost, but you have been found.

Endnotes

All Bible verse quotations were done using the New King James Version unless otherwise noted.

Chapter 1: Our Neuron Trees

1. R. Hetu, 'AI Can Be A Central Nervous System', *Gartner*, Stamford, CT, Gartner, Inc., 2019, https://blogs.gartner.com/robert-hetu/ai-can-be-a-central-nervous-system, (accessed 5/27/2021).

2. G. Markowsky, 'Physiology', *Britannica*, Chicago, IL, Encyclopedia Britannica, Inc., 2017, https://www.britannica.com/science/information-theory/Physiology, (accessed 5/27/2021).

3. B. Voytek, 'Brain Metrics: How measuring brain biology can explain the phenomena of mind', *Scitable*, Cambridge, MA, Nature Education, 2013, https://www.nature.com/scitable/blog/brain-metrics/are_there_really_as_many/, (accessed 5/27/2021).

4. P. Reber, 'What Is the Memory Capacity of the Human Brain?', *Scientific American*, New York, NY, Scientific American, 2010, https://www.scientificamerican.com/article/what-is-the-memory-capacity/, (accessed 5/27/2021).

Chapter 2: Be the Tree You're Meant to Be

1. 'Salvator Mundi (Leonardo)', *Wikipedia*, Wikimedia Foundation, Inc., 2021, https://en.wikipedia.org/wiki/Salvator_Mundi_(Leonardo), (accessed 5/27/2021).

2. 'Know thyself', *Wikipedia*, Wikimedia Foundation, Inc., 2021, https://en.wikipedia.org/wiki/Know_thyself, (accessed 5/27/2021).

3. P. Mckenna, 'Butterflies remember caterpillar experiences', *New Scientist*, New Scientist Ltd., 2008, https://www.newscientist.com/article/dn13412-butterflies-remember-caterpillar-experiences/, (accessed 5/27/2021).

Chapter 3: Body, Soul, and Spirit Connection

1. S. Joshi, 'The body: Memory transference in organ transplant recipients', *NAMAH Journal*, Sri Aurobindo Society, 24 April 2011, 19 (1), https://www.namahjournal.com/doc/Actual/Memory-transference-in-organ-transplant-recipients-vol-19-iss-1.html, (accessed 5/27/2021).

2. A. Herold, 'Neurogenic Tremor Through Tre Tension, Stress and Trauma Releasing Exercises According to D. Berceli in the Treatment of Post-Traumatic Stress Disorder PTSD', *Trauma Prevention*, 2015, 2 (1-2): page 4. https://

traumaprevention.com/wp-content/uploads/2018/04/pscp_2015_2_1-2_9.pdf, (accessed 5/27/2021).

Chapter 4: The Cognitive Model: Tapping Into Our Brain Trees

1. M. Pearce and others, 'Religiously Integrated Cognitive Behavioral Therapy: A New Method of Treatment for Major Depression in Patients with Chronic Medical Illness', *NCBI*, Bethesda, MD, National Center for Biotechnology Information, 3 Nov 2014, https://www.ncbi.nlm.nih.gov/pmc/articles/PMC4457450/, (accessed 5/27/2021).

Chapter 6: Rest in this Truth: You are Accepted, Not Separate

1. T. Johnson, 'Getting to know the Center for the Study of Global Christianity', *YouTube*, Gordon-Conwell Theological Seminary, 14 Feb 2017, https://www.youtube.com/watch?v=NJnorTNc5YM&t=82s, (accessed 5/27/2021).

2. Translated by P.E. Pusey, 'Cyril of Alexandria, Commentary on John, Book 1', *The Tertullian Project*, Ipswich, UK, Roger Pearse, 2005, https://www.tertullian.org/fathers/cyril_on_john_01_book1.htm, (accessed 5/27/2021).

Chapter 16: Obsessive Compulsive Disorder

1. 'PTSD Clinical Practice Guideline: What is Exposure Therapy?', *APA*, Washington DC, American Psychological Association, July 2017, https://www.apa.org/ptsd-guideline/patients-and-families/exposure-therapy, (accessed 5/27/2021).

Chapter 17: Depression: The Big Black Dog

1. M. Johnstone, 'I had a black dog, his name was depression', *Youtube*, World Health Organization, 2 Oct 2012, https://www.youtube.com/watch?v=XiCrniLQGYc&t=2s, (accessed 5/27/2021).

2. 'The Home of Cognitive Behavior Therapy and Recovery-Oriented Cognitive Therapy', *Beck Institute*, Bala Cynwyd, PA, Beck Institute For Cognitive Behavior Therapy, 2021, https://beckinstitute.org/, (accessed 5/27/2021).

Chapter 23: Build Resilience

1. R. Kipling, 'If', *Poetry Foundation*, https://www.poetryfoundation.org/poems/46473/if---, (accessed 5/27/2021).

Chapter 24: He Swallowed Death in Victory

1. S. Wittman and M. Shaiman, *The Place Where Lost Things Go*, Walt Disney Music Company, 2018.

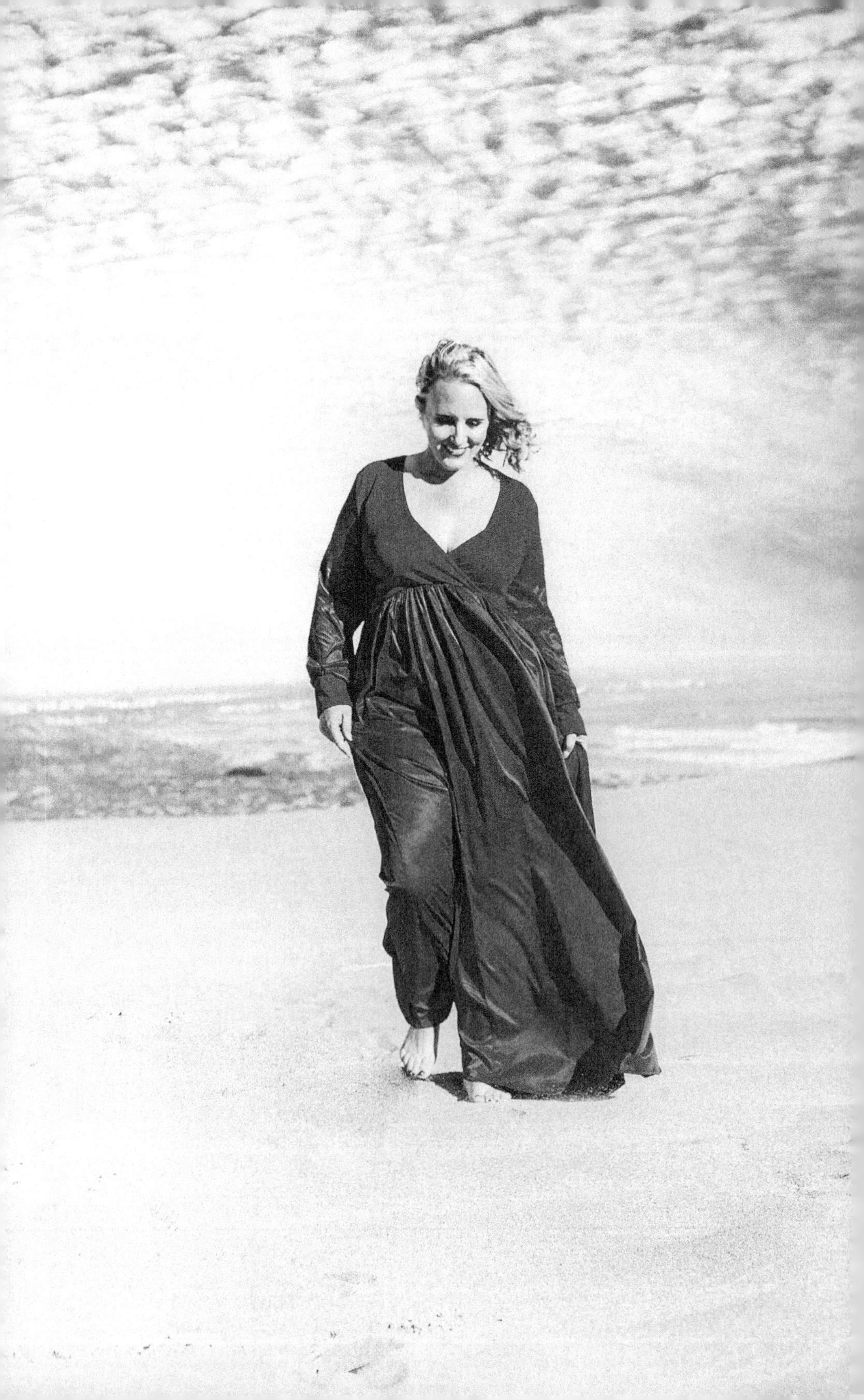

About the Author

Amelia Mathee has dealt with thousands of people thirsting for answers. Her counseling approach incorporates both her knowledge in the fields of psychology and neuroscience as well as her biblical understanding—this is where Scripture meets science. Even though you may be "wired" one way, you can begin the journey to rewire your brain and find that oasis after all.

Maybe you're feeling alone in the desert and don't know which way to turn. This is your opportunity to choose a new life for yourself. "This is what I do," says Amelia. "I meet people in their desert, and I help them find their way out."

Seraph Creative
Heaven's Heart for Earth

Seraph Creative is a collective of artists, writers, theologians & illustrators who desire to see the body of Christ grow into full maturity, walking in their inheritance as Sons Of God on the Earth.

Sign up to our newsletter to know about the release of new books.

Visit our website :

www.seraphcreative.org

Printed in Great Britain
by Amazon